A Gift of My Own

A Journey Into the Spiritual Realm of Reality

Josie Giuseppa Basile

BALBOA.
PRESS

A DIVISION OF HAY HOUSE

ISBN: 978-1-4525-3979-9 (sc)
ISBN: 978-1-4525-3980-5 (e)
ISBN: 978-1-4525-3981-2 (hc)
Library of Congress Control Number: 2011917035

Balboa Press books may be ordered through booksellers or by contacting:

Balboa Press
A Division of Hay House
1663 Liberty Drive
Bloomington, IN 47403
www.balboapress.com
1-(877) 407-4847

Printed in the United States of America

Balboa Press rev. date: 10/24/2011

This book is dedicated to my
friend and mentor Joseph Fioravanti

and my spiritual guide
Katherine Marshall of course.

ACKNOWLEDGEMENTS

There are many people who have contributed and enriched my life. Thank you for your words of wisdom, your loyal support, and being the voice in my head. You are all FIRST.

Joseph Fioravanti, 12/01/1927-7/20/2009, my friend and mentor. You read my first full manuscript and said, "There is a voice in this book that wants to be heard." You encouraged me more than you will ever know.

Thank you ***Rosa Ruffino Brindley*** for your blind faith and belief in the cause. You TOO were called. You were the wind beneath my wings.

I am grateful to you ***Marianne Gallina Loduca*** for reading the chapters as I was completing them. You said, "You are holding back. The reader will know that. Don't be afraid, just let it go." You were right. I was wrestling with this dilemma. You were the voice in my head.

A very first thank you also goes to my brother, **Francesco Basile**. As I was writing each chapter I was e-mailing them to you. You called me up one day complaining, "You left me in suspense. I haven't received any chapters in a while." This was my first realization that I might have something special.

A very special thanks to **Kathyanna Marshall Bagnardi**. You edited my first draft. You said, "I enjoyed reading it and editing it so much. I read the manuscript three times and learned something new each time." Thank you also for sharing your mother, **Katherine**.

Thank you **Wendy Saldriaga**—You reaffirmed what I needed

to hear. "I have never read a book before, soooo, don't be offended if I don't finish reading your book. I started reading it Saturday morning and only intended to read a few pages. I couldn't stop reading it! I only took time out to fix myself a sandwich. When someone called I got annoyed."

Thank you **Holly Martin** for that beautiful poem you wrote after reading the book. You said words that inspired me, "I went on this journey with you. I cried and I laughed."

Connie Storey—How can I possibly thank you. You came to my aid at one of the lowest points in my life. I don't know what I would have done without you that night.

Ardith Louise Dinga, my editor and friend who I nicknamed—Eagle Eyes. You TOO were called. There are no words for my gratitude. You inspire me with your belief in this book. You also insisted on reading the manuscript out-loud three times together—Eagle Eyes.

Big thanks to you both, **Elizabeth and Dr. Paul Koenig**, for your support and love, at one of the lowest points in my life. **Elizabeth**, you are the yang in my life. Your love and loyal support has been a gift. You have opened my world to so many wonderful new experiences.

Another first is my sister-in-law **Marianne Gallina Basile.** You made me face the reality of this book. I read the book for the first time out loud to you. You and I were both amazed at what was written.

What can I say to you, my friend **Maureen Bailey**. You are the ying in my life. You are a true friend. I love you – I will miss you now that you are moving to Florida. Our laughter still rings in my home as we worked on the house projects on those memorable weekends. You were there encouraging me on to write this book.

A very special thanks to **Mama and Papa, Maria, Francesco Basile**, for your never failing love and support.

To my children **Albert Hecker**, his wife-**Bridgette,** my darling granddaughter, **Ayla Louise**, and my precious daughter **Dr. Louise Hecker** for being the love and light on the journey of my life.

A hearty thankfulness to my fellow travelers in India from the State University at Oneonta, Learn & Serve Program: **Heather Mason, Jennifer Borst, Esmahan Zuccar, Bipina Patel, Amber Rehling, Maegan Lee, Patrick Hickey, Luke Mahoney, Aaron Hunter, John Wickett, Professors-Ashok Malhotra and Suzanne Miller.** I am grateful for the multitude of unique experiences we shared. We will always have India and the Indo-International School.

CONTENTS

INTRODUCTION

Early in my marriage I had an experience that shifted my perception into an unknown direction. My husband William and I were in New York City, a weekend get away, from the sleepy town of Oneonta, in upstate New York. It was late November and the air was crisp. The anticipation of Christmas was in the air. The city streets were full of people, bustling about in the steady fast pace for which New Yorkers are known. The steady rhythm of my heels joined the steady beat of the symphony. The bright sun and the cool air felt refreshing as I snuggled in my warm black mink coat.

We stopped at the curb waiting for the traffic light to change. I noticed the crowd parting on the opposite side of the street, leaving room for a dubious intruder approaching the curb. He was pushing a shopping cart and I knew that in it were his worldly possessions.

The light changed and the intrusive looking man started crossing the street. He was stooped over, pushing his cart, and walking in a slow methodical stroll. He gazed straight ahead with a non-committal look. He was tall, husky, with a ruddy complexion. He had a long Roman nose, droopy cheeks and eyes. His dark hair was down to his shoulders. He was wearing a long dark brown overcoat that drooped to the top of his black rubber boots, the kind you wear over shoes. They had four metal straps in front, unsnapped.

As we approached, I looked up and our eyes locked for a split second. I felt a jolt; I was startled and quickly looked away. There was compassion, love, and peace in his eyes. I felt as though it was I who was the intruder in *his* world.

As we passed, I turned and looked back. His boots caught my eye. There was a slit on the heel of both boots, flapping open as he steadily plodded on. I could see bright, pink, clean skin exposed as he lifted his feet. It was as though those feet did not belong on the body of this man.

"William," I said, "let's buy that man a pair of shoes." William jerked at my elbow to keep me moving. I looked back, but the crowd had engulfed the stranger.

Even though this encounter lasted only a few minutes, the experience has stayed a lifetime. I have thought of that man often over the years and have sent him bouquets of prayers and good wishes. I vowed to God that day that I would never pass a fellowman that was in need, and asked Him to use me when He needed me. Those thoughts and that vow would change the course of my life and place me on a path that I never could have imagined. This was my calling card and a sign post along the path of my life.

I have since understood that this man was on his journey, seeking his truth, and walking his walk. Perhaps he was there as a symbol that my journey was about to begin. My journey is part of a larger plan and greater than I am.

I could not have known that the life that I knew would soon fall apart, and the most incredible journey was about to begin. The path I have traveled has been intriguing, amazing, wondrous, and an expression of love for humanity. Experiencing the mystical essence of God left me with the desire to want and understand more. This wonder would take me to three countries on three continents. This new path, which I reluctantly entered, opened new worlds that exist within the reality of spiritual continuum. What my eyes could not perceive, my soul revealed. My heart was opened and it expanded my realm of spirituality. Thus began my searching within, which took me on a journey without.

FORWARD

I did not want to write this book and put it off for many years, until I could no longer contain the Inner Voice. Many times in my writing, I did not want to express certain aspects of my journey. However, I was not able to contain the Inner Voice; I surrendered, bared my soul, told all, and released, A Gift of My Own. The fulfillment of my journey was not complete until I had written this book. Additionally, it will join and enhance the broader spiritual consciousness that has awakened in the world.

By Divine intervention, I have been given the amazing responsibility to bring forth A Gift of My Own. This book is part of the gift that will keep on giving. I am only a bit player and very insignificant in the scheme of things.

A Gift of My Own is for you, for the individual who is searching for your own messages and awakening. For the individual who is ready to receive the call to the gift, this will connect and fan that spark of divinity. This might be your calling card.

I know that somehow A Gift of My Own will fall into the hands of the people who are meant to be touched. This book will fall off the shelf, stick out, catch your eye, or a friend may give it to you.

Please pass this book on. It is not meant to be held, but to be shared.

Section 1

TRUTH RESIDES IN EVERY HUMAN HEART,
AND ONE HAS TO SEARCH FOR IT THERE
AND TO BE GUIDED BY TRUTH AS ONE
SEES IT. BUT NO ONE HAS A RIGHT TO
COERCE OTHERS TO ACT ACCORDING
TO HIS OWN VIEW OF TRUTH.

Mahatma Gandhi

LESSONS FROM DEATH AND BEYOND

I was in the presence of a woman I had known as a child; her name was Katherine. She had been one of the cafeteria workers at the school I attended with her daughter, Anna.

Katherine walked with a limp, a deformity from birth. Katherine was slender, with porcelain skin and dark short hair. Her eyes were a warm brown and her voice was kind and tender. Many times I did not have the thirty-five cents to pay for lunch. Katherine would just nod and write the charge on a sheet without embarrassing me or allowing other students to know. When mama cashed the milk check, I would quietly slip Katherine the money I owed for my brother, sister, and me.

Her daughter Anna and I were best friends. We grew up together in a small farm village called Grand Gorge in the Catskill Mountains of New York. Mama, Papa, Rosa, Antonio, and I immigrated to America when I was seven, from Carini, Italy to Brooklyn. Four years later, I was running through the fields on a 350-acre farm. Growing up on the farm during the turbulent sixties, the Viet Nam War, and the outside world, seemed like a distant drum.

Katherine made me feel welcome in their home. Anna and I were able to discuss with her various situations that kids have at that age. Eating American food in their home was a treat for me. Being an Italian immigrant, mama only knew how to cook Italian food.

Anna and I had recently graduated from high school when her mother, Katherine, died of cancer. I grieved her death like I would have a member of my own family. She had been a mother figure in my young life and someone I had loved and trusted.

It was now ten years after her death and I was face to face with Katherine. I understood that I was having a dream and that I had transcended into another reality while in a dream state. I was aware that she was no longer in my world; and yet, I was seeing Katherine. There was an acceptance of seeing her and I had no fear in her presence. I have since understood that fear is a human emotion. Since I was in the spirit realm, there was immediate acceptance and acknowledgment of what I was experiencing.

It was white around us, misty like clouds, which extended far beyond any boundaries. There was nothing visually distinctive other than Katherine. She looked the same as when I had known her as a young girl, healthy, vibrant, and young. She stood a few feet in front of me. I saw her only from the waist up. Even though I do not recall her opening her mouth, we conversed.

Katherine said, "Give Anna a message for me. Tell her everything is going to be all right."

"Why not give her the message yourself?" I asked with inquisitiveness and wonder.

She answered with a comforting and familiar voice, "Anna would be afraid if I went to her." I internally accepted her response and settled my inquisitiveness.

I thought, this is a perfect time for me to ask her questions since she is no longer in my world. She knows the answers that I wonder about. The first question that came to my mind and a universal question that humankind ponders at one time or another, "Is there a ___". I had not finished thinking the question when she directly answered me.

"Yes, there is a God."

"What's God like?" I asked.

"Not the way you imagine Him to be."

At once, before she had finished her words, I felt a vibration of warmth within and a feeling of immenseness. It was as though

4

there were no boundaries or barriers that could contain this feeling of joy. I was humbled by the experience. I internally understood—this is the True God, which transcends humankind's capability to comprehend.

The perception I had of God when I was growing up was that of a grandfatherly man, with a white beard, ready to judge, condemn, and throw me into the depths of hell. This image was now immediately dispelled. I could not dwell upon this inner feeling because there were other questions I wanted answers to.

Another universal question that seekers of Truth want to know, "Is there a Heaven?"

"Yes," she said, "there is a Heaven."

"What's Heaven like?" I asked with wonder.

"It's like the gypsies' secret," Katherine said.

There was an internal grasp to her statement of *the gypsies' secret*. I will never understand Heaven until I become part of that world. Human words cannot make clear the unexplainable things that pertain to the spirit world. Heaven is indescribable, incredible, joyful, and a wondrous place to be. Yet, there are limitations to these mere mortal words because heaven is much more.

Something stopped me from asking her any more questions about Heaven and God.

I have often asked friends what they think *the gypsies' secret* means. They have not been able to give an adequate answer, to which I instantaneously understood. The gypsies are cloaked in mystery and are a closed society. They have a lifestyle and culture that defies society's perception and penetration. There is a saying, "If you ask twelve gypsies the same question, you will hear twelve different answers. If you ask one gypsy the same question twelve times, you will hear twelve different versions." So it is with heaven. There is no one definitive answer because there are numerous versions of the same question.

I woke up and could not believe what I had just experienced. As I lay there in bed, I felt dizzy. I could still feel the glow of love vibrating deep within. There was awareness that my experience with Katherine had not been a dream. I can only explain it as I had been there with her and now I was back. I had been fully conscious and responsive to what I had been experiencing during my dream state. I knew that I had connected to another reality, which is as real as the one I live in.

I was aware that I had spent time conversing with Katherine and understood that this was not the time for me to remember the particulars of our conversation. It would be years before my soul would reveal the secrets and the amazing experiences of the path that was before me. At this time, I would not have been able to grasp the events had I remembered our conversation. But my soul understood that my time had come for my journey to begin.

This was the beginning of these amazing insights.

My first reaction was, why me? A humbling question I would ask of myself many times in the years to come.

I called Anna. I felt an urgency and obligation to give her the message. I did not have time to think or explain what I had experienced. I simply blurted out, "Anna, I have a message for you from your mother. She told me to tell you that everything will be all right."

I could hear Anna crying softly on the phone. She said, "I would like to hear more. Let's get together this Saturday."

We did not have time to go into depth with explanations or answers at that time. Anna is a teacher and was on her way to school.

It never occurred to me that she would not believe me. Only afterwards I voiced to myself, "She must think I am nuts!"

Anna and I had remained close over the years. We would periodically get together for lunch. I knew how her mother's death had been a tragic loss in her life and one she had never gotten over. Ann's father, Justin, died a few years after her mom. Anna was still numb with pain from her mother's death when her father died.

When Anna came to visit, to my surprise she said, "I have been waiting for an answer from my mother and asking for assistance with my personal problems." She then asked a question that I had also asked of her mother, "Why didn't my mother come to me instead of you?"

I gave her the answer that her mother had given me. "You would be scared."

"I would not have been scared," she said. "I would have loved to have seen her."

I did not know how to reply. I had no answers that could satisfy her pain. I was perplexed as well.

Both of us put this experience aside for many years. It would come up in our conversation at times, but we did not really dwell upon it because there seemed to be no adequate response to Anna's question.

Years later, Anna and I met for coffee and she again brought up the dream of her mother only this time she really got into her personal problems and was much more reflective on her life. She told me she had gotten pregnant shortly after that dream and found the connection that she had been searching for.

She questioned again the fact that her mother had come to me instead of her. I had questioned myself as well over the years. "Anna, I can only give you the answer that your mother gave me."

"I understand that, but I feel so disappointed that I didn't see her."

It was as though the answer to respond to Anna was suddenly readily available to me now.

"You must understand, your mother knows you, and perhaps if you had come face to face with her you might have become engulfed with pain at seeing her and missed the message. Giving the message to me had a greater impact because you still remember her words. You were asking for assistance and the only way she could answer you was to let you know that she heard you. That comforted you."

"That's true," Anna said.

"There could be other reasons, as well," I said. "You may have dismissed it as only a dream and forgotten it years ago."

"You're right," Anna said, "I most likely would have forgotten that dream. Over the years I have recalled her words and they have comforted me and I have felt her presence during those times." Anna now had the answers that took away the grief of not seeing her mother. Her questioning was over.

I felt that there were other reasons that Katherine came to me, besides comforting Anna.

For reasons yet unknown, a porthole within me had opened, after the experience with Katherine. She had been there to help me enter a world of questioning, self-doubt, wonderment, spirituality, and extraordinary insights. This mystical experience left me with a desire to search for more knowledge and a longing to feel that personal and immense love.

I was spiritually, emotionally, and mentally stimulated to search for understanding and Truth. This did not diminish with time. I became receptive and open to the unknown. I had no idea where my search would take me and it was uncomfortable. How could I have understood that Katherine had come to open and prepare the way, years before the actual journey began. I never could have anticipated the awareness, which in time would be revealed.

THE GENIE OUT OF THE BOTTLE

There was an internal understanding that something monumental had occurred from the experience I had with Katherine. I could not forget it. I had internal knowledge that an adventurous journey was waiting for me and all I had to do was cross the threshold of the porthole that opened before me.

A door had been unlocked and I had peeked through. I became consumed with the desire to understand and to experience that intense feeling of spiritual love. It was as though a genie wanted to be uncorked and I could not contain it.

There was a feeling that I would be safe while being guided to knowledge that was readily available. I could not grasp nor deny this inner urgency and bewilderment. I did not want it, but the desire to enter was greater. This began my struggle to venture into the spiritual realm while at the same time wanting to close the door. This was a paradox in my being; my soul and my mind seemed to be in battle for control.

Venturing out of my safe hibernation was uncomfortable and painful. I knew that I could not hide in the safe cocoon forever. I reluctantly and begrudgingly was released to thought provoking questions. I longed for answers.

Can the dead return and give information to the loved ones they have left behind? Do they see us whenever they want to? Can they help us at times of need? Where are they? Where is Heaven? Where is Hell? Is there a Hell?

While I had this insatiable desire for inner knowledge, I also begged for guidance and forgiveness, if I was wrong in my wandering and questioning. My Catholic upbringing did not leave room for questioning; absolute acceptance was expected. I was laboring under the teachings of my childhood. I began the struggle of believing with faith, or accepting the questioning and doubts within me. I trusted and I feared at the same time.

Once I started to question, I knew I had crossed the threshold and had gone through the open door. I seemed to have a new awareness. This felt as though veils had been removed from my inner eyes. I was seeing and understanding more clearly. I was open and observed with a diverse perception. I felt vulnerable but had assistance from within.

An internal contradiction and battle began. *If God is Love, then how can there be hell? Is God a vindictive spiritual being who will condemn an individual into hell for eternity? What is bad and who set the standards for being good? Why do most religions not mention purgatory; a place between heaven and hell to work off ones sins?*

Why would God throw Adam and Eve out of heaven when He knew they were going to eat from the forbidden fruit? After all He is God and He knows what was going to happen, so why this drama? What was the devil doing in heaven? Is there a devil? Why would God allow man to fall when He knew the result?

I went around and around in my questioning. My inner core was shaken with questions that I had never dared to think about before. I had been taught that these thoughts were wrong and I would go to hell for having them.

Even though these thoughts were fear provoking, there was calmness within the core of my being. There was an understanding that I did not know the whole truth concerning the true God.

Religion had asked me to accept its teachings with absolute faith. My inner voice seemed to say, "This does not mean the acceptance of false perceptions and teachings." This new consciousness perplexed me.

I could no longer accept my religion without question; it was as though I was hungry all the time, while the table in front of me was full of food. I could not touch it, eat it, nor question it. The fact that the food was there should have been enough to fill my needs. I had experienced the love of the true God and that awakened my desires to want and know more. These feelings and questions provoked me to continue the search for answers.

I became receptive to greater understanding. I felt that all the answers were there for me and all I had to do was ask the questions before retrieving a response. It was as though I had to step aside within myself for spirituality and knowledge to grow.

I recognized truth because it seemed to vibrate and resonate in my soul and this was a liberating emotion. This felt similar to an awareness and remembrance of what was Truth. Once I understood that I understood Truth, I knew it had been there all along and was now within my grasp. My spirit within seemed to be vibrating with knowledge and love. This felt as though a connection had been reestablished.

The human aspect of me, or my ego, seemed to have stepped aside during these occurrences. This felt as though the ego and the spirit could not occupy the same space and time within me. The spiritual side of me would eventually win out.

It was not long before I became aware that the binds of organized religion were being released from my soul. This was a very lonely and devastating path to be on. I had to let go of something old and familiar in order to allow and accept new knowledge to come in.

I read books to find any connections to my own experiences. One of the first books I came across was, _Seth Speaks_ by Jane Roberts, published by Bantam Books. Seth is an entity that crosses over to speak through Jane and is transcribed by her husband, Rob. This book connected with me and opened up my inner core of understanding. The book pointed out opinions that I understood unequivocally. This is my interpretation: _With the last human breath we exhale, our soul energy slips out of our body,_ *and into another existence which the soul immediately recognizes as being home. This existence is as real as the one I am now living in. The soul acknowledges, after this transition, that the journey on earth has been completed and that the goals set before leaving have been accomplished. Once the soul energy enters the spiritual existence, it still can reenter earth's realm through dreams, apparitions, vibrations, or thoughts in the minds of loved ones left behind.*

These things I acknowledged because it felt as a remembrance, a feeling deep within me, now being recalled, understood, and placed in the forefront.

I did not spend all my time searching for answers. I continued to live my life and then I would feel this tug within me. It's as though I was pulling on one end of the rope not wanting to venture in, while the other side was pulling on the other end of the rope saying, "It's time, come on in. You have more things to learn. Hurry up!"

I would become consumed with a deep aching feeling, the longing to know more, and the only way to quench this desire was to give in. This would draw me back to search for understanding. Once I had understood the new knowledge, I would then get on with my life as though nothing had happened, until the next tug, which would connect with the previous spiritual experience. The tug would present itself in many different ways. It was as though something would happen or come before me, to present me with the next step in my spiritual growth.

I struggled with every change in my life to an unusual extent; even though I felt that the change was necessary for my progression. Eventually I understood what was happening and I acknowledged the struggle.

At times, I felt like a spectator in my own life. I was smaller than the events that I was experiencing. I did not fully belong in either place, my everyday life or in my spiritual existence. Eventually these things did not confuse me. There was an acceptance of these thoughts and feelings.

I felt guided and protected, but who was guiding me and for what? It would be years before I would understand. This was *'the calling to the gift'*.

Spirituality eventually transcended my religion. Slowly and methodically, I felt like an onion being peeled away as I searched in order to reach the core, the essence of Truth. I became less fearful and more bold with my questioning, venturing out into audacious questions. *Could religions be in the infant stage of understanding the factual relationship of God and humanity? Could Truth have been lost in the numerous translations and deletions in order to accommodate the survival of humanity with the concept of organized religion? Have the roles been reversed? Is humanity now keeping organized religions alive? Has the time now come to get back to basics and the truth, to look within for the answers instead of without?*

I thought of my own religion and how it had changed over the years to accommodate the ever-changing society. *How can a sin be considered in one century, and yet, not in another? How many millions of Catholics have died thinking they were going to hell because they had eaten meat instead of fish on Friday?* Now, it is *no longer a sin. The Pope revised this religious rule in order to help the economy of the Italian fishermen. How lax religions have become with the condemnation of divorce as more and more families become victims. The rules that were once inflexible have now become obsolete.*

I was starting to see religion in a new light and it scared me. *Have religions become moral judges? Isn't God the only one that can judge us? Does He judge us?'*

I did not know whom to turn to for help with my questions. At this time, I also started searching for people who could read tarot cards; in the hopes that they could give answers to questions I had in my personal life.

It was in these early years of experimenting that my friend Connie recommended that I go see a woman to have my tarot cards read. She assured me that this woman was very good at predicting the future. I had become skeptical after having gone to other tarot card readers who had given generic answers that could apply to anyone. I had no idea where my life was going; however, I thought someone had to have answers for me.

I met the woman that Connie suggested and felt a connection to her. She was young, in her mid thirties. At first she did not say anything to me. She placed a cup of tea in front of me and asked me to drink it. I obeyed without even questioning why. I did not know that she read tea leaves. I was waiting for her to pull out the tarot cards.

When I finished my tea, she took the cup and looked inside; I looked too. With both our heads together, looking in, I could see a million speckles of tea leaves around the inside of the cup. She said, "You are going to shed many tears. I have never seen so many tears. Yet, there is something else I have never seen; a wooden staff is next to you. You have power and help from up above."

What is she talking about I thought. What powers could I possibly have? I already have shed plenty of tears. She must be wrong in these predictions. Even though I inwardly questioned her words, they sank like a heavy stone to the depths of my soul. I knew she had tapped into information that would make sense to me in time. I pondered that experience for weeks. I begged God to take that cup away, but I knew it was waiting for me.

I continued to have a connection to the spirit world. I became open to more experiences in the dream reality. I had encounters of seeing my dead grandparents in my dreams. I understood that they would be attending upcoming family events. I accepted these experiences, even though I knew it was unusual to have them. I refrained from telling details and only partially told Mama and Anna. How could I tell my cousin Joey that I had dreamed our dead Nonno (grandfather) Giuseppe would be coming to Joey's wedding along with other dead relatives? However, with time, I dismissed the experiences. I did not dwell on them.

During these experiences, I was aware that I was in the spirit world. There was no room for doubt that I was in their reality. In most dreams, one visualizes oneself in them. I did not see myself in these dreams because I was part of that reality. I could see how they looked and what they wore, but I did not see myself other then the fact that I was in their presence. During these dreams, I was looking and speaking directly to my dead family members.

There was inner knowledge why my relatives came to my dream: They do not forget us once they are gone from this earth. The love is the attachment, which connects both existences. They do not come to help us, because they cannot interfere. They come to see how we have grown and evolved from when they were part of our lives. These experiences and encounters went on for years. In the meantime, I was struggling to hold a marriage together.

MY NIGHTMARE

I did not devote all my time to searching for truth because I was living a nightmarish existence.

I met William, my husband, on May 23, 1969, when I was a college student at Delhi State University, a two-year technical college. I was taking business and secretarial courses.

My roommate Kris and I were out for a walk when we stopped to pick lilacs. I later learned that William and his cousin Donnie were in the shrubs drinking blackberry brandy. They knew we had to return that way from our walk, so they waited to initiate a meeting with us.

William was tall with blond hair, green eyes, and dimples. He and his family had just moved from Queens to Delhi, New York. He was finishing his last year at the high school. I was finishing my first year at Delhi College.

At five foot two, a cascade of auburn hair, brown innocent eyes and disposition, William was intrigued with me. That September he joined me on campus, studying to be a lab technician. We fell in love.

It wasn't long before I realized that William was drinking, cutting classes, and lying to me in relation to his whereabouts. I broke up with him a few times, but somehow we reconciled. William would always promise that he would change and I believed him.

In 1970, I graduated and started working at Delhi College as a secretary.

We set our wedding date and made future plans. William

would run my brother Tony's college bar, in a small town called Cobleskill. We were going to save our money so William could continue his studies. He had not graduated; he had cut too many classes.

A few weeks before our wedding, William's mother, Louise, asked me to come and see her. She begged me to get William out of the bar. "He will turn out to be like his Uncle Gene, if you don't. He was an alcoholic, ran around with women, and died in a bar room brawl."

"It's only going to be for a short time," I said. "I promise I will get him out as soon as I can."

Three years, three months, and three days from the day we met, William and I were married at the Sacred Heart Church in Stamford, New York. From the money we had saved from the two of us working, we had a wonderful honeymoon being tourists in Italy.

We spent a week in Rome and Florence and then flew down to Sicily to visit my hometown of Carini. I had not visited since I had left as a child. It was thrilling to see my cousins, aunts, and uncles. We stayed with Zia Rosa and Zio Croce in Carini.

We returned from our honeymoon and William started working at the Vault, the college bar, in Cobleskill. William's mother died four months later, from cancer, on New Year's Eve, December 31, 1972.

William started coming home drunk from the moment he started working at the bar. He was like a kid in a candy store. In this condition, William would become abusive, verbally and physically. The thought of leaving occurred to me but how could I admit failure to my family and friends? I was just married. I was ashamed. I was in love. I could not believe this nightmare was happening to me. William was a wonderful person, when he was not drunk. I did not know at the time that he was drinking a bottle of whiskey, Black Velvet, every night. No one knew the demons I was dealing with. This was the scope of our first two years of marriage.

Mama and Papa bought a corner building in Oneonta, New York. They opened an Italian restaurant in one section of the building and called it Mama Nina's. There was one empty spot with an apartment above it. William and I knew that he had to get out of the bar and into something else. Since there was no seafood sold in the Oneonta area, William and I decided to open a fish market and moved into the apartment above. Anything I thought, as long as he got out of the bar. We knew nothing about seafood. September of 1974, two years from when we were married, we opened the Oneonta Fish Market.

I worked in the market with William. We created a good clientele. He was not drinking, that I was aware of that year. The following September I gave birth to a son, Albert. I stopped working to raise our son. William worked downstairs. I was able to go up and down the stairs to keep an eye on things and on William. Life seemed good. We were thrilled with our beautiful blond haired, brown-eyed, dimpled son.

The business was flourishing. We put in fryers and started selling take out seafood. We again expanded, moved things around, and put in booths to accommodate the expanding business.

Then I started noticing a pattern. Every two to three weeks William would create a verbal altercation, storm out, and come home drunk. It finally occurred to me that William might be an alcoholic; however, he did not get drunk every day. How could that be I wondered?

In time, I learned that there were various degrees of alcoholics. William could refrain from getting drunk every day, but eventually it would reach a point where he needed to get the high of being drunk. He would make promises of never drinking AGAIN and I believed him. The nightmare continued.

I soon realized that I was on edge and always waiting and wondering for the next binge to take place. It was almost a relief when it did happen because I could relax for a while. It was a chaotic existence, never knowing when it would occur, or what would happen.

Two years after our son was born, I gave birth to a beautiful daughter, Louise. She was dark haired, fair skinned, with big blue eyes. When Louise was six months old and Albert was two, we moved into my dream home.

I was happy to get out of the one bedroom apartment and move into a four bedroom raised ranch, on a hill overlooking the city of Oneonta, on a sprawling five-acre lot. The house has two fireplaces, a family room, living room, dining room, kitchen, and four bathrooms. Our furniture seemed lost in the new home. This was a perfect setting to raise our children. Now, I thought, William will change. We have two children, a home, a business, and with this comes responsibilities.

His drinking seemed to have gotten worse. I was not there above the restaurant to monitor his drinking. Many nights I paced the living room floor watching for the car headlights to turn into the driveway, waiting, wondering what condition he would be in. Many nights I would rush to bed and pretend to be asleep in order to avoid an argument.

At moments of despair, I would look up and whisper to God, "Where are you—why don't you help me? Change him or take him away." What a lonely, painful existence I lived in.

Like most alcoholic relationships, I kept silent. I was too ashamed to confide in anyone. To have revealed this information would be to admit that my picture-perfect marriage was a lie. There seemed to be no answers but to deal with the pain in silence.

When Louise was a year old and Albert was two and a half, I placed them in nursery school and went back to work with William in what was now a prosperous little restaurant and seafood market. We applied to obtain a beer and wine license. To our surprise the beer license was granted but not the wine. Apparently, there was a law that prohibited the selling of wine within two hundred feet of a church. Various churches surrounded us.

"No one who battles with the Liquor Authority ever wins," I was told repeatedly. This became a crusade, a challenge, and I had to win at something.

After five years of personally fighting the Liquor Authority, the law was changed. Restaurants could now serve wine and beer within 200 feet of a church. I had solicited Republican Senator James Seward. He had attached the liquor law change to another bill and the New York State Senate and Assembly voted it into law. The State liquor authority had not known that it had passed into law until I went and applied for the license again. Only this time I mailed the application in with a copy of the signed bill from Mario Cuomo, which Senator Seward had given me. It never occurred to me how it had affected the rest of New York State until my cousin Bella, a few months later, applied for a wine and beer license in Staten Island, for her restaurant called Basile's. Across the street from Basile's Restaurant was a church within 200 feet. When she received her rejection letter, she called them up and said, "You better check your laws. My cousin, in upstate New York changed this law." The realization that I had affected the lives and businesses of many in New York State amazed me. How could I have known that this would be nothing compared to the lives I would touch on the other side of the world.

It was a hollow victory. What I had won had nothing to do with William's drinking. He was going to drink anyway. This was my battle for the restaurant and for me. At times, I could not help to wonder at the irony of the whole thing.

When Louise was four and Albert was six, we bought a restaurant that had previously gone out of business. William thought it was a great opportunity. It had a bar. William was determined on obtaining this restaurant. I could not persuade him and I had no choice but to support the decision. William convinced me that he would not drink and I wanted to believe him. I was that naive. We called it, The Captain's Table Restaurant.

William came home drunk often. Our life continued to be mayhem. I wanted to believe that there were reasons for this turmoil continuing in my life but I could not find or accept any explanation. It was at this time that I had my spiritual experience with Katherine. It is surprising that I did not ask Katherine any questions about my marriage. The questions I asked her were in preparation for my opening into spirituality. My soul was connecting on that level. This may not have been my plan, but according to my spirituality, I was following the progression that I was meant to follow.

My spirituality and my life seemed to co-exist side by side but did not overlap or interact. It was as though the two did not have an association, other than the fact that it was happening to the same person, me. The spiritual experiences were forgotten after they occurred. I did not dwell on them. My life was a nightmare and my spiritual experiences had no connection, or so I thought.

THE CROSS

Eventually, William was picked up for drunk driving and written up in our local newspaper. Oneonta is a small community; everyone knows everyone and I had become a small town celebrity with various articles in the local paper for my fight with the Liquor Authority. I had dealt with his drinking in private but now it was open to public scrutiny. I felt that everyone was looking at me and judging me. William would hide in the kitchen of the restaurant; he cooked the line and supervised the kitchen staff, while I dealt with the public. I was in front at the restaurant, taking reservations, managing the dining room, scheduling, and training the service staff.

I still kept silent with the pain of his drinking. Our family life was being torn apart. My heart was being chipped away bit by bit by the anguish of William's behavior.

Louise and Albert were ten and twelve years old by now. They understood what was going on. They encouraged me to leave their father. Louise would beg, "Leave him mom. We will go with you."

Why didn't I leave? A question I am sure women ask of themselves when they stay in a bad situation. There are as numerous reasons as there are situations. My reasons seem very insignificant now. I did not have the strength to leave. Where would I go? I was humiliated and had conformed to that way of life. How could I admit failure? I had no way to provide for my children and myself. Habit? Perhaps the most irrational reason of all, I still loved him.

My Italian upbringing of staying with the husband, regardless of circumstances, certainly played a big part.

At times of pain, I would continue to reach out to God and plead, "Where are you God? Change him or take him from me."

The bad publicity in the local paper was damaging to our restaurant business. Now the public was reading of William's drunk driving episodes and no longer coming in for dinner. Since we were business people in the community, the newspaper went into details concerning William's drunken driving accident. At one point, I went to see the editor of the newspaper and begged him not to write about William's last drunk driving incident. He had hit an electric pole, flipped over the vehicle, and totaled it. The editor knew us well. He said to me, "If William is that stupid, that he continues to drink and drive, then, he deserves to be written up."

At this time, also, a woman, while crossing the street from the restaurant parking lot on her way to the restaurant, was killed by a passing car. The newspapers wrote numerous articles that the parking lot had inadequate lighting.

The business continued to lose patrons. We had no choice but to try to sell the Captain's Table Restaurant.

I kept questioning God, "How could you do this to us? We had worked so hard." If this could happen to us, then there can't possibly be a God. Maybe I was being punished for having questioned my religion, but then why not punish just me instead of my family?

It was agonizing not knowing my family's future. I had put so much into that business and so had William. Even though William would be out of the bar environment, when we sold the restaurant, I knew that it really did not matter. Somehow, someway, the drinking would continue. I had dealt with so much pain in my life, this was another failure. How much more could I possibly handle, I wondered.

I was feeling let down. I felt alone, abandoned, and empty deep within. I did not have the strength to stop the spiral of empty feelings. It was an agonizing pain in a hollow well of darkness and it was closing in on me. I wanted to reach out to God but did not understand how I could. It was as though the pain I had experienced in my marriage and the failure of the business were entangled into one massive question, "Why God—how much failure and pain can I possibly take?" I wanted to let go of the last shred of hope within me that kept pushing its way into my consciousness, "Could there be a reason for this happening?"

Then it happened. One night I had a dream reality that I was at the foot of a cross. I looked up and knew it was Jesus. It was black all around, just the cross and me. Jesus' head was tilted to the right side, bent down toward His chest. I could not see His face. Suddenly I saw slithering up the cross, going around and around, a serpentine—like creature, nothing I had ever seen before. It was not of my world. I felt calm and watched with wonder and inquisitiveness.

As the creature was getting closer to Jesus' head, I heard myself inwardly saying, "It is going to bite Jesus." As the creature got ready to strike, at that instant, Jesus slowly lifted up His head and tilted it in the direction of the creature, towards His left. I watched the creature, as it started falling and then dissipate before it reached the ground and my feet.

I looked up at Jesus' face. He was looking down at me. In a calm comforting voice He said, "Have faith in me."

I was startled awake! I was in awe. Jesus came to *me* and asked *me* to have faith in Him? Was it possible? There was that familiar connection that it had been an experience in another reality with the familiar magical feeling.

Yet, I thought to myself; did I make this dream up because I needed some consolation for what was happening in my life? Did I create this drama so I could accept the spiral I felt I was in? Was I creating an excuse for my own benefit? Was it too simplistic to say that Jesus had come to my dream to comfort me? Was I, in my subconscious mind, creating this scenario because of my vulnerability? Did this really happen?'

I felt deep within that the experience was real. I was making excuses not to believe this extraordinary mystical encounter. I so desperately wanted to understand this occurrence. There had to be an explanation to this amazing event. I had to connect to someone or some thing.

I went to the church that morning, in hopes of finding some solace. I walked down the full length of the church. It was quiet, no one was there. All I could hear was the clanging of my shoes on the marble floor.

I stood in front of the large altar and looked at the back wall. There was a large golden cross with a white marble statue of Jesus nailed to it under a blue canopy. I looked intently at the cross, not knowing what to do, now that I was there.

I begged God for understanding. Questions were still bombarding my mind. Did Jesus really come to me? Things like this do not happen to ordinary people like me . . . or do they? Why would Jesus take the time to single me out when there are more complex problems in the world? I am nobody, nothing, it could not have happened. I must have imagined the reality of this experience.

The cross was far away and appeared small from where I stood. I took off my shoes and walked up the three steps onto the altar. The marble floor felt cool on my bare feet. I felt meek and sheepish; I had never done that before. It seemed sacrilegious. I felt that I was walking on hallowed ground.

I walked the full length of the altar and stood underneath the canopy. I tilted my head back and looked up. I gasped; it was the same face and position as had been in my dream. His head was tilted to the right and down towards his chest. I looked closer and realized His features were the same and I was in the same position as I had been in my dream.

I started questioning myself again. 'No, God could not have come to me. Could that really have happened? That is impossible or is it? Why would He come to me? No, it couldn't be.

Suddenly a strange thing happened. The cross came to life—it grew large and took up the whole wall. The cross-radiated light; and yet, light came from above, and shone brightly on the cross. The figure on the cross underwent metamorphosis. It pulsated from skeletal bones to a covering of flesh. The cycle went back and forth in a blinking flash, repeatedly.

I covered my eyes and thought—This cannot be happening. I must be imagining it. I do not believe it. It cannot be true. I don't want it to be true.

I did not trust what I was seeing. I peeked between my fingers and looked up—it was still flashing instantly back and forth, from flesh to bones. I was not scared, just overwhelmed with both disbelief and acceptance.

"Have faith in me," whispered within me. My questions had been answered. I felt compelled to leave.

I walked off the altar very slowly, still amazed and in awe with the experience. I sat on the steps, put on my shoes, but kept my head down. I could see that the light was still bright. I did not look up at the cross as I rounded the corner and up to the front of the altar. I was humbled.

I walked slowly down the full length of the church and up to the front door. Cautiously and slowly I turned my head and looked over my shoulder and up at the cross. It was still radiating and flashing back and forth from flesh to bones.

I walked out into the bright sunshine. I was filled with love, peace, and further questions, but the agony in my soul had vanished.

There was no fear within me for what I had just witnessed. How can there be fear in the presence of God. Love and fear do not co-exist at the same time.

There are no adequate words that can explain the feeling of

what I had just experienced. There was acceptance that Jesus had come to give me a message. I understood there were reasons for this happening and in time I would know them.

I said to myself, "Yes Lord; I will have faith in you. I have no idea where my family is going or what is going to happen to my marriage but I will have faith in you".

I had no idea that my path was being cleared and a new journey was about to begin. I did not have the courage or the wisdom to understand this at the time. Walking in the path with conviction is not always one of assurance and certainty. Even with these experiences, I still wondered and questioned. "I hope you know what you are doing God, because I certainly don't."

I struggled to maintain my belief. I begged His help to maintain my faith. When I would reach the point of despair, I would recall my cross experience. Then I would ask myself, "Why would God take the time to come to me, when I am just an ordinary person among many? God must have other things in this world to think about, than just one single person as me?" It was a calming affect on me to stop, question, and wonder. It's as though these thoughts were there for me to explore and ponder.

God did have his reasons but I would not know them for years to come.

ANGELS

Perhaps selling the restaurant might be a blessing in disguise, I thought. We went back to working in the fish market. A year later, we sold that as well. We had enough money for me to take a year off before venturing out and making any decisions on what job I could do. Since I had spent my adult life working with William in the restaurant business, I had not utilized my secretarial skills. Time had not stood still and my skills were obsolete. There were computers now, something I knew nothing about.

William was working for a food company located in Albany, an hour away from home. He would call restaurants in the surrounding area and take their orders for various foods and supplies. William was very good, because of his background in the restaurant business. He could anticipate what the restaurants needed. He would call in his orders to the company in Albany and the company would deliver them. He only reported once a week to the company in Albany. William's driving license had been suspended, for another drunken conviction. For a while, I had to drive him to work in Albany. I would go to the park, read, and wait underneath a tree for William to get off work. I was unfamiliar with the Albany area, so I did not venture out. William's drinking was curtailed during this time period. He no longer had the freedom or excuses to be out late drinking with the employees. I was no longer pacing the floor, waiting, watching for the headlights to turn up our driveway. Life seemed to have some normalcy.

My sister-in-law, Lee, encouraged me to join her in the sale of real-estate. Her mother was the owner of DeMulder Realty, for Better Homes and Gardens. Before I knew it, she had me enrolled in taking classes to obtain my real-estate license. I was soon selling and listing homes. I was thrilled to see myself doing something on my own.

By this time William started working for another food company, also in sales. He had his driver's license back and drove to Albany every day.

One morning I received a phone call to list a house, twenty minutes from the office, in Cooperstown. My gas tank was low and I was out of checks. I was unfamiliar with debit cards and ATM's. They were not as prevalent as they are now. I always had cash flow because of the businesses. I was embarrassed to ask anyone in the office to lend me money for gas. I thought I needed checks to do the transactions. It never occurred to me that there were other means, and perhaps I was not meant to know.

The real-estate office was in a converted old railroad station with a large parking lot. My desk was the last one in the open, long, and spacious room. I was sitting at my desk and looking out the window and whispered to myself, "God, I need ten dollars, five for gas and five to have in my pocket. You have never let me down before. I can't believe you will let me down now." I said it with faith, humbleness, and fevering belief.

After I said those words, I spotted two old men walking in the parking lot. My inquisitiveness peaked as I watched them carrying a large clear plastic bag, which I could see, was filled with empty cans and bottles. They placed it near where my car was parked.

It was like watching two elves at work on Christmas Eve. They wore long overcoats, open in the front. It was the middle of March and the weather was somewhat warm for that time of year. I watched as the tall man waited by the bag, while the shorter man waddled into the building. He stopped at the secretary's desk and I watched him as he walked to the first agent's desk. He then continued crisscrossing the room from desk to desk, apparently speaking to each agent. I saw all the agents shaking their head as if to say, "No . . . ."

He finally came to my desk. He spoke in a mumbled and incoherent manner; yet his voice was very clear and distinct to me. "I was at the railroad track and picked up these bottles and . . ." It was as though I internally heard what was being said without hearing the actual words. It was apparent what he wanted, to be taken to the grocery store. I replied without waiting for the rest of the sentence and was already getting up, "No problem, I will take you."

He said, "I will pay you for this."

"Don't worry about it." I knew I could not take money from two homeless men. On my way out the door, I informed the office manager that I was going to get the listing in Cooperstown. I do not know why I even said that because I still did not have the money for gas.

I went to my car and placed the bag in my trunk. Neither man said a word to each other. The tall man stood by the car, with a big smile on his face, as the shorter man got in the front seat next to me.

I looked at the tall old man as I pulled away. He bent down, looked at me in the open car window, and waved with a warm comforting smile.

I looked back, as I pulled out into the street, and saw that he was still standing there smiling, following the car with his eyes and waved at me again. I had absorbed his face and eyes. He was tall with fair skin and had the most incredible warm blue eyes. I felt a connection to that man; it yanked at me and I could not understand why. Yet, I cannot describe the old man that sat next to me in the car. His face has remained a blank.

As I started to drive away, I thought, this man is going to stink. I took a sniff and realized that he did not. As I silently drove, my mind wandered back to my immediate problem and I thought, this is stupid, here I am in need of gas and I am wasting gas!

30

As soon as I thought those words, my passenger said, "Don't worry about it, I will pay you for this".

Even though he had mumbled those words, I again heard him loud and clear.

I nonchalantly said, "Yea, yea", and just drove. It was as though he heard my thoughts but I did not think anything of it at the time.

When we arrived at the grocery store, I placed the bag on a shopping cart. I motioned at a boy who was gathering carts to take that cart into the store. I went to my car lost in thoughts and suddenly realized I had not said good-bye to the old man. As I turned to look for him, I found him right behind me, and I was pinned in the open car door. He opened his wallet and practically placed the open wallet under my nose; it was full of money. He plucked one of the bills, shoved it at me, and turned away. It happened so fast that I did not have time to argue or say anything. I was stunned and frozen to the spot, as I watched him slowly walk away and disappear into the store. I got in the car and sat there for a moment. I slowly opened my hand to see how much he had given me. I was astonished to realize that he had given me a twenty-dollar bill.

At a gas station, I filled up with ten dollars' worth of gas and put ten dollars in my pocket. As I was driving, all of a sudden the incident that had occurred replayed in my mind. I could not believe it. I received twice what I had asked for and in such an inconceivable way.

What in the world just happened—had God answered my prayers, I wondered. I was in awe to say the least. I was struck by the simplicity of what had occurred. Could they have been angels, I wondered. There was a magic feeling inside of me that I could not grasp.

When I got back to the real-estate office from Cooperstown, I still had that magical feeling. I do not recall if I got the listing on the house. I slowly walked to my desk, looking at each agent as I passed his or her desk. I wanted them to inquire about the old man. No one looked up to speak or ask about him. There was an unusual pin-drop-quietness in the office. I stomped my feet even louder as I walked down the aisle, in the hopes that someone would look up, and at least ask about the listing. It was a scoop to obtain a listing in Cooperstown and the procedure would have been to inquire. I had discussed the listing at the meeting that morning.

I wondered, didn't they see me walk out with the old man? I think they did. Did it happen? Of course it happened; I still have ten dollars in my pocket.

I wanted to inquire of the people in the office if they had seen the old man, but something prevented me from asking. The words stuck in my throat and couldn't come out. It was as though the incident had never occurred and I was the only one that knew that it had. I was dumbfounded by this unusual experience.

I soon realized that they had been bit players in this extraordinary occurrence and they did not know it. The experience was for me and not for them.

I spent the next four years in that office with the vision of those two old men out in the parking lot. Every so often, I would walk behind the building, look up and down the railroad track, and search for empty bottles or cans that might have been tossed. I never saw one. Since commercial locomotives went by, that was not likely to happen, but it still did not stop me from looking.

I live in a small community and always looked for the old men; yet, I never saw them again.

Out of curiosity, I eventually filled up a clear large garbage bag with cans and bottles, similar to the one the two old men had. I took it to the same grocery store to see how much money I would get. It came to four dollars and change. As usual, I was astonished. There was no doubt in my mind that the experience had been a response to my plea.

In time, I accepted the knowledge that angels had visited me.

After that I read many stories about angel's coming and doing God's work on earth. Angel Letters by Sophy Burnham tells of angel stories from various people in various situations. It seemed that everyone's story that I read was comparable to mine.

The stories all relayed the fact that angels appear at times of crisis and disappear when their work is done. They come in human form. They present themselves in many disguises, representing various people, to fit the situation and circumstances. They will speak through other people to give answers, support, knowledge, and comfort. Not believing in angels can prevent their intervention and the feeling that something amazing and magical has occurred.

In these stories, angel intervention was rarely recognized while it was happening. It is as though, the spirit does not allow that knowledge to be known at the time that it is occurring. It is only afterwards, when reviewing the experience and trying to understand the occurrence, that one realizes the events cannot be rationalized. There is an internal feeling, without doubt, of the mystical implication. The experience is humbling and feels miraculous.

As each new experience occurred in my life, I would somehow find the right book, which would acknowledge and give clarification to my experience. I was now looking and becoming aware of clues that were being presented to me. I was open to the universe and the universe was preparing me for what I was about to embark on, changes that would transform me completely and place me on a different path. Still, with all the awareness and experiences, I was always open to wonderment and awe. The child within was always present.

As I read more, it seemed that I was being prepared for more. I had such a connection with and in God; and yet, I was not ready at all for what was to happen in my life. There is no way that I could have known, that this was only the beginning of my experiences with angels.

THE CRUISE

January, 1993, was an exciting time for me. William and I were going on a Mexican cruise, a real vacation for seven days.

A few months before the cruise trip, I said to William, "For once, can't we have a holiday season, without you being drunk?"

On board ship he said to me, "Did you notice that I didn't get drunk during the holidays?"

I looked at him in astonishment and thought, isn't that the way it's supposed to be? I whispered, "Thanks." The awareness that he could stop himself from getting drunk had never occurred to me. If he could do that once, why couldn't he do it again and forever, I wondered.

During the course of the trip, it was announced, that the captain of the ship would be performing a group ceremony for people who wanted to renew their wedding vows. I kept hoping for a new beginning and I thought that by renewing our vows this could be what we needed. I was an optimist. William was reluctant, but agreed to do it to please me.

The morning of the ceremony, as I was waking up, I felt a strange sadness come over me. It was as though a light was going out, with gloom filling me. I sat up in bed and felt this unexplainable shadow literally drop on my head, as though an egg had been cracked. It slowly moved down my body, covering every inch, as it spread the feeling of sadness. This was an intense feeling.

I cried throughout the renewing of vows ceremony. I could

not understand nor stop the despair I felt. I could not shake the melancholy feeling for the rest of the trip.

We got home from the trip and I pushed those feelings behind me. But the feeling of sorrow had left it's residue within me. Occasionally, throughout that year, I would feel that unexplainable sadness and for a second it would consume me. I quickly would whisper a vigorous, "No, go away!" I did not want that feeling to continue.

William was working for the Cisco Food Company, for four years by this time. The episodes of his drunkenness were less severe, although, the dinner table became a battleground. He was brazen and argumentative with the kids and me. He would go over the same thoughts, repeatedly, such as reprimanding the kids, or complaining about something that happened at work. When I would question him as to why he was behaving as though he were drunk, after only one glass of wine at dinner, he would snap back at me, "I am tired."

"So am I, but I am not slurring my words." I later found out that he would buy a pint of Peppermint Schnapps from the liquor store and drink it before getting home. He would be chewing gum when he got home and I, of course, thought it was the gum odor.

I was busy listing and selling real-estate. I felt that I had found my niche. I really loved what I was doing. I was doing something on my own, with great success.

Louise was fifteen at this time. Her long cascade of dark curls framed her beautiful face and big blue eyes. Louise is outspoken and did not back down from William, a combustible combination. She is tall and athletic and a straight A student. I recall how she came home from school one day and went straight to her bedroom without saying a word to me. I asked Albert, "What happened?"

"I don't know mom. She was quiet on the drive home."

Albert and I knocked on her door and I asked, "What's wrong Lou?"

Her tearful response was, "I got an eighty-five in Science."

Albert whispered, "I would be thrilled to have gotten an eighty-five."

Albert was seventeen. His blond hair, dark eyes and the flashing of his dimples made him very popular with the young girls. The phone never stopped ringing for either of them.

Louise and Albert were as different as night and day. They were best friends, but on completely different levels when it came to their priorities in school.

One day Louise and Albert came home and handed me their report cards; a short computer printout of their grades. I made a fuss over Albert's report card. He was passing everything. He was very nonchalant over the whole thing. Louise was unusually quiet. Of course, her grades were great.

I could not let go of the fact that Albert had done so well on his report card. A few days later, I called Albert's guidance counselor to see if there was something we could do to continue this unexpected good report card. The guidance counselor laughed and said, "Are we talking about the same Albert? Why don't you come in and let's take a look at it."

Albert had fabricated his grades by printing out both report cards, so they would look the same. He did not have to change Louise's grades.

I was the primary care giver for my children. I tried to stay involved in what they were doing in school and who their friends were. It always seemed to be the three of us against the world, especially when dealing with their father. They were good kids and I wanted to give them so much more than our present life. The emotional pain that William was causing our children was tormenting me. The situation had not changed over the years and we were coming up to twenty-one years of marriage.

THE GIFT

At the beginning of September of the same year as the cruise, I had a dream, which bewildered me. Like before, there was a knowing that this experience was actually happening in another reality, in a dream state.

I found myself on the side of a dirt road, in a kneeling and squatting position. It was predawn and I could barely see shadows. I was scared and tried to crouch down even lower. I was fully conscious of the emotions I was feeling.

I whispered in a desperate voice, "God wake me up . . . . Get me out of here . . . . I am scared . . . . I don't want to be here."

Suddenly, two figures in brown robes with hoods appeared, walking slowly towards me. They stopped before me and extended a hand. They spoke in a unison singsong voice, "We have been waiting for you."

They had such sweet and comforting voices. The fears within me dissipated. I extended my hands, reached toward them, and found myself walking between them. I could not see their faces. I felt safe and protected. There was a recognizable feeling that they were angels.

At once, we came to a large castle door. With my left hand, I pushed the door open. I experienced the familiar radiance of love that opened before me. No adequate words can describe the intensity of this feeling. There was a brilliant white inside the castle door, although, it was not hard on my eyes. There were no walls or boundaries; the radiance extended out and beyond.

Inside sitting at a round table, which had a white tablecloth reaching the ground, was an old man with a white beard and long white hair, wearing a white robe.

I stood in the doorway and was instantly taking all this in. I could not move. I understood that I was on another level, on the edge of his world, and it was not the time for me to enter.

The old man was sitting at the side of the table, looking at me. Our eyes locked. They were full of compassion and love. He spoke to me without moving his mouth and said in a tender and soothing voice, "I have a gift for you."

I was startled awake after hearing those words. They seemed to have penetrated me. I was stunned by this new revelation. There seemed to be an arousing within me, but there was serenity at the core of my being.

I would repeat the words, "I have a gift for you", over and over again. It seemed as though the words would echo inside of me, like a tuning fork and then calmness would follow.

I told Mama, whom else could I possibly tell, "I have a gift coming from God. What could that be?"

Then I started questioning. What could God possibly give me? Something was coming—what could that be? What did He mean?'

Then the doubts started creeping in. Was it God? Who was that person that was going to give me a gift? Would God come to me and tell me that He had a gift for me? I fought between believing and disbelieving. The doubting, however, could not take away the elated emotion within me while sensing that something significant was about to happen. How could I possibly have known that I would soon come crashing down.

A few days after the dream, Louise and I went shopping in Albany. After our shopping spree, Louise and I went to William's office to say good-bye before heading for home. The time was around four in the afternoon. It would be hours before William was expected home.

As we sat in the lobby waiting, the receptionist said, "He is working late tonight".

I looked at her trying to grasp what she meant. I finally asked, "What time does he usually leave?"

"Around three," she said.

I felt an alarm going off inside of me.

William hurriedly came out to the lobby and kissed us good-bye. He mumbled something about having things to do before leaving for home.

Driving home, Louise, and I sat next to each other in somber quietness. She finally turned to me and said, "Face it mom, Papa is having an affair". She said it so effortlessly, without emotion. She voiced what I had not dared consider.

"How can you say that about your father?" I said sternly.

That night William denied and defended his stance. "You never trust me. You are imagining things." The rest of that month was full of arguments.

"Lord," I kept begging, "what is going on?"

One night I had a dream. I was at a busy railroad station, standing on the train platform, waiting for it to leave. Everything was foggy, mixed with the train smoke. The train whistle blew and then I saw William with a petite blonde-haired woman. Her features were a blur. I had a pail, of what I knew, was filled with bleach. I splashed them with the bleach and then immediately woke up.

I told William of my dream. He said, "That wasn't nice."

"What?" I asked. His comment did not make sense.

That evening at the dinner table, I was enlisting William's support in dealing with a problematic issue concerning the kids. He sat there not saying a word. He ignored the situation. I looked at him and nodded as if to say, "Help me here."

He looked at me and shrugged his shoulders as if to say, "I don't care. It's your problem." I was perplexed.

I dealt with the everyday issues of my teenage kids. I rarely enlisted William's help. His idea of disciplining the kids was swearing and threatening to hit them. The mere mention that I was going to tell their father was enough to get the result I wanted.

A few days later, the end of September, William announced that he needed time to be by himself and would stay in Albany during the week. He said that he was tired of all the arguments at home and of driving back and forth from work. He would be home early that Friday for Louise's swim meet.

I knew that he had been acting irrationally, even for William. I was sure he was having some kind of mental problem. I was distraught!

I called my friend Connie, who lived in Albany, and explained the situation of William being in Albany. She tried to comfort me. I could not be consoled nor understand what was going on. I had been brainwashed by William that I was imagining things and that I had no reason not to trust him. I did not believe what would have seemed clear to others.

I lived for Friday to come. I sat on the bleachers at the school, looking and waiting for William to show up. The swim meet was over and still William was not home. I made a phone call to two hotels in Albany. He was registered at the hotel we had stayed in that previous January, before we left for our early flight to catch the cruise ship. The hotel confirmed that he had not checked out and had reservations for the following week. No one answered when they rang his room.

I called Connie, explained the situation, and informed her that I was driving up there to make sure that William was in stable condition. She said, "Take my phone number in case you need me."

I was driving on highway I-88 and thought that perhaps it was a bad idea. William would be furious, saying that I did not trust him. I turned around and headed for home.

However I felt this urge to get back on the highway, and I

headed towards Albany again. I again talked myself out of it, turned around, and headed for home. I was fighting the impulses that were tormenting me—should I go—should I stay. I got back on the highway for a third time and this time stayed headed towards Albany.

At the hotel I saw William's car parked in the parking lot. I went to the desk clerk, informed him that I was William's wife, and needed his room number and key. It is rather amazing that he gave them to me.

I knocked at his door and said a few times, "William, it's me, open up." No answer. I tried the key but it would not open.

I went outside and called out to William at the first floor window, next to where his car was parked. I was sure this was his room, from the location of where I had tried the hotel key. I stood on tiptoes and tried to look in the room. The drapes were drawn.

I went to the front desk and said to the clerk, "The key won't work, something is wrong."

He went with me. He said, "The door is double locked. Someone is in there. I saw a shadow in the peep hole."

I was sure that William was having a nervous breakdown and would not open the door. He must still be angry with me for even questioning his decision to be in Albany, I thought.

I brought the hotel clerk outside, to look at the window, to see if there was a way for me to get in. I noticed the car was missing and the curtain was blowing in the wind.

I asked the clerk if I could climb in the window to get in. He shrugged his shoulders as if to say, "I don't care."

The clerk left and I scrambled up the window and slid onto the floor. As I sat on the floor, I quickly looked around and said, "Oh my God. I am in the wrong room." In the open coat rack were women's clothing hanging up.

As I stood up, I noticed familiar clothing; William's suits were hanging there as well. The reality of what was going on in that room could not be denied. Everything seemed to become in slow motion and I was trying to feel my way, as though I was in a thick fog. I was in survival mode.

I pulled down her clothing. They did not belong next to my husband's clothes. I looked at his suits still hanging there, anger welling up in me, and I tore them down too. I looked around not knowing what to do. There was a small table set up for coffee. I threw coffee and coffee grounds on their clothes. I dumped creamers and juice on them. I put a hairdryer in the toilet. I smashed her watch with my shoe. I tore the sheets off the bed. I was numb, in a daze, and in slow motion.

I called Connie. The extent of our conversation, which I remember, was Connie saying, "Stay there. I'm on my way."

I waited in front of the hotel for what seemed to be an eternity. I collapsed in Connie's arms when she reached me. I was still in that foggy feeling of slow motion.

"I destroyed the room," I said.

"I want to see it."

She laughed when she saw it. She came out of the bathroom with a glass of water and said, "Take this, it will help you." Connie was a nurse.

She took me to her home and fixed a bed for me on her couch. I sat up all night, looking out the window in a numb stupor.

I called William the following morning and said, "Did you have fun?"

He said, "Yea, did you?" After a long pause he said, "I will be home this afternoon."

My drive home seemed endless that morning. I screamed and cried all the way. "God," I wailed, "this is my gift? Couldn't you think of something better? When I asked you to change him or take him away, I did not think you would really take him away. I did not know I had to specify which choice I wanted. I was sure you knew."

By the time I got home, I was hoarse from all the screaming.

Passing cars must have thought I was insane. For once, I knew that I *was sane*. It was almost a relief to know that.

I was composed by afternoon when William walked in. He stood on one side of the kitchen counter, while I stood on the other side facing him. "Well," I said, my voice still hoarse from all the screaming, "is she a real blond?"

He smirked. "Now you know."

"Now I know."

"You made a mess out of that room. We stayed up all night cleaning it."

"Am I supposed to feel bad about that?" There was a long silence between us. "We can

work through this," I said, forever an optimist.

"*Now* we can work through this? You have never forgiven me for Cobleskill."

"You never left Cobleskill. You have always had one foot in our marriage and one foot out." He paused and stared at me, as those words seemed to penetrate him.

"Why couldn't you have left things alone? Why do you always have to be so inquisitive?" he asked.

"Living with you has made me that way."

"I have crossed the line. I have no choice but to move forward," William said. "You can never forgive me. I will be moving to Albany. She has nothing to do with it. It is something I have to do."

"Someday I will thank you for this," I said, not believing a word that came out of my sore throat. "You will have to tell the kids."

When Louise and Albert came home, we sat at the kitchen table and William said, "I am leaving your mother and moving to Albany."

Albert said, "*You're* leaving mom? She should have left you ten years ago."

"She probably should have."

"You didn't ask if we want to go with you." Albert asked in anger and pain.

"Well, do you?"

"No, but you didn't ask."

Louise looked at me with sadness in her eyes, as if to say, "I am sorry that I was right."

This is the ultimate pain, betrayal. I was inconsolable. I lashed out at God. "How could you allow this to happen to me? What did I do to deserve this? So this is my gift, you destroyed my marriage and my life?'

I was angry with God. Begging I would whisper, "Where are you God?" I struggled to maintain my faith. I begged to not let me lose my faith in Him. Even with all my spiritual experiences, it still would have been easy to let go of the belief that there was a God.

I tried to lean on God but that was shaky and weak. "Please help me to hold on to believe in you," I begged. I was hanging on with a sliver of hope, that there were reasons for this happening to me.

Darkness and gloom, which I had felt nine months earlier on the cruise ship, was within me. I was there now and was falling into the agony of darkness within my soul, and it would not let up. When I would reach a point of anguish and hopelessness, unusual thoughts would enter—"Someday I will be grateful that this happened and all these tears will turn to joy." Deep within I would hear, "Be not afraid—this too shall pass." Those words and thoughts were like a beacon of light, showing me the way out of darkness. Moments of pain and despair would be set back. Day by day, the darkness was occurring less and less.

Somehow, I knew these inner words I was hearing were truths, because they came from the depth of my being. Yet I wondered, how can that possibly be? How can I be grateful for this pain in my life? How can I ever laugh again?

I grieved all the pain I had experienced in the twenty-one years of our marriage. I mourned the loss, failure, and disappointment of the happy-ever-after illusion.

One day Louse and Albert sat on each side of me on the couch and said, "Mom, you cry all the time. What can we do to help you?" I heard what they were saying and not saying. In my anguish I had lost sight of the fact that their world had fallen apart too. They needed me. They were looking to me for strength and stability. I had to get myself together for their sake as well as mine.

I had lost my identity. I was no longer a wife, which had identified me. My splintered life ached with the uncertainty of my future. I felt broken in every sense of the word. I had no idea whom to turn to. No one seemed to be there to help me or to understand the struggles I was experiencing.

The best I got from my family and friends, "You will be fine; you're strong".

Those words seemed meaningless but they made me stop and think. What did they see that I didn't see? Could they possibly be right?

I sat next to a friend, Jeannie, at Louise's swim meet. "Jeannie," I said, "my husband walked out on my family."

She looked at me square in the eyes and said in her southern drawl, "How old are you?"

"Forty-two." This seemed to be a rather odd question to ask after I had told her that my world had fallen apart.

"Perfect," she said, "not too young, not too old. You will create a brand new life."

How can this be perfect? How can anything be perfect after this? I did not understand why I had the feeling of acknowledgment of her words. Those words would echo in my mind, many times.

The words that had reverberated in my soul and had been foretold years earlier were acknowledged. "So these are the buckets of tears I would cry."

I have since understood that I had been trying to control what

I thought I wanted, even if it was a bad situation. Being an Italian Catholic, there was an unspoken rule that women were to stay with their husbands, regardless of circumstances. I was going to be a divorced woman and carry a big D on my chest, for the rest of my life. I was a failure.

If it had been my choice, I would have stayed in the abusive and unhappy marriage, rather than wander into the unknown and uncertainty of life.

My driving to Albany and finding William in the hotel room had to occur in order to free myself to move forward. I had to see with my own eyes, in order to accept, the reality of my marriage, which was a shamble.

God had better plans for my life. How could I have known that the call to the gift was blossoming. In order to move to the next level, my path had to be cleared.

My brother Tony, his wife Mariana, and teenage children, Frank, Croce, and Maria, were going to Italy in March for Easter, to visit our family in Carini, Sicily. Our sister Rosa and husband Giovanni went back to Italy to live years earlier with their children, Rosa, Croce, and Valeria. We also had aunts, uncles, and cousins there whom had never moved to America.

Tony encouraged me to join them. I thought it was a good idea. Louise and Albert encouraged me as well, "Go mom. It will be good for you."

Perhaps, visiting my roots will help me I thought.

MY ROOTS

Touching the soil of my birth, after months of turbulence and pain, was very emotional. Memories of childhood flooded me as I recaptured feelings of innocence, love, and wonder. Walking the cobblestones, as I had done as a child and as generations before me had, my tears were flowing, but soon dissolved.

I recalled what Mama and Papa had told me of the anomaly which occurred on the day of my birth. A blizzard hit tropical Sicily that March. Three feet of snow fell overnight. This was something that they had never seen or heard of happening before or since. In that part of Italy, people were not accustomed to snow; it only hailed occasionally. This became a joyful event as people of all ages took to the streets, throwing snowballs, making snowmen, playing, and laughing at this unusual weather.

I was born in a house, as most children were at that time in Italy. The law regarding newborns was that fathers were to register the child on the day that they are born, or pay a fine for each day missed. Because of the unusual event of snow, the day of my birth was registered days later at the municipal building. Papa, I am sure, did not have the few liras to pay for the days missed. He registered my birth on the day he went, which was March 12. Mama and Papa, to this day, still argue as to the exact date I was born. Mama's argument is, "I was there I should know."

Of course Papa would answer back, "So was I. That's why I should remember."

When I was two years old, children in the village were dying from whooping cough. I was playing outside, splashing in the fountain when Mama heard the horrible sound of that cough. She and Papa immediately took the bus and rushed me to the nearest hospital in Palermo. The doctor gave me twenty-four hours to live. At the stroke of midnight, I sat up in bed and said, "I am hungry. I want some bread." I was in the hospital a few weeks before Mama and Papa could take me home.

As I walked aimlessly around the village, feeling those familiar cobblestones beneath my feet, I wondered why I had survived. So many children at that time had died. I could not help but wonder, could there be reasons?

I visited the house I had lived in and put my hands in the fountain that I had spent many hours playing and splashing in. There is a castle behind the house and it has since become famous because of its history and the movies that have been made there. This castle was featured in the movie, *The God Father* three.

I went into the alleyway and tried to get into the castle as I had done as a child. I recalled standing at the window, on tiptoes, watching the horse and motorcycle races below on the winding road. The castle was now locked and being turned into a museum.

Papa had been a milkman with one cow. I could envision Papa walking his cow and stopping at different homes. I would stand by our house and wait my turn for Papa to fill my cup with milk. The realization that we had been poor was intriguing. It had never occurred to me before. Everyone in the village was like us.

I visited the church and remembered how Zia (Aunt) Rosa would give us a lira to go to the movie next door to her house. Every group of streets had its own small community church. With Zia Rosa's lira, my brother and sister, along with my cousins, would sit on the floor in a small back room of the church. It was a makeshift theater with a sheet hung up for a screen. It may not have been much but it was great for us kids. This was the only movie theater we knew.

The episodes of leaving our home in Italy and coming to

America flashed before me. They had been engraved in my young mind. I sat on Nonna (grandmother) Rosa's lap on the car trip to Palermo. Everyone was quiet and very subdued. Nonna quietly and with a quivering voice said to Mama, "Now you won't forget to write", as she choked back tears. It would be the last time that I was in Nonna Rosa's arms and the last words I would remember her saying. She died five years later. We did not know about telephones. How could anyone explain to us what a phone was, since we had never seen one and I am sure no one we knew had one? Years would pass before we had a phone in America.

As I walked the cobblestone streets and walked by where Nonno (grandfather) Giuseppe and Nonna Rosa had lived, I recalled the last time I had seen them together. Papa, Mama, Rosetta, Antonio, and I had stood on the top deck of the ship Sathunia, waving at Zia, Zio, cousins, Nonno Giuseppe and Nonna Rosa below us. I felt the first pangs of pain in the separation. As I clung to Mama's dress and looked at those familiar faces below, she and I wailed with tears. I did not fully understand what America was, but at that moment, I did not want to go there. I wanted to stay where I was because it was what I had always known. It was easier to hang on to something I knew than to wander into the unknown. How could I have understood that America was a wonderful place where I would experience incredible new things like telephones, television, movie theaters, washing machines, dryers and a million other things? How can one understand what one has not seen or experienced?

We left for America on Christmas Eve. I was six years old. I wore a short blue shawl, which my great Zia Christina had knitted, and a shear light blue dress. My sister Rosetta would turn four on board ship. She wore a pink shawl with a shear pink dress. These would be the same clothes we would wear when we got off the ship in New York City, January 4th. They were not adequate for the bitter cold winters of Brooklyn.

As I walked around Carini, I recalled some memorable

moments of our journey from the ship. It had stopped in Portugal before going out to the open sea. Papa got off the ship to look around. Mama, Rosetta, Antonio, who was nine, and I waited for Papa on the top deck for his return. I recalled looking down on to the pier and noticed a photographer taking pictures of us. It would be a picture of a beautiful slim young woman, with auburn hair, light porcelain skin, and somber green eyes, standing next to three young well behaved children. I have always thought that Mama looked like the actress Maureen O'Hara. Mama was only 27 years old. Looking back now, we must have seemed like the typical immigrant family going to a new world.

I can still see Papa among the crowd on the pier below, with a branch of bananas on his shoulder. Papa had one American dime left in his pocket and had used it to buy bananas for his young family. They were a novelty for us, an amazing treat. Papa certainly had a strong resemblance to young, thin, John F. Kennedy. Young handsome Papa was 33 years old and taking his young family to an unknown country. The money Papa had gotten for selling the cow and the few pieces of furniture we had in Carini, had paid for the boat trip and the new shoes we all wore. I am certain the relatives in America had also contributed for our journey.

There was an aroma on board ship, which has never left me that I would inhale as we walked toward the dining room where we had our meals. It was a very pungent, unique, strong aroma with the mixture of various foods all in one. Every once in a while, I will still get a whiff of that particular odor when I walk by a diner, and I am instantly transported back to the ship, Sathunia.

As our ship got closer to the harbor in America, I recall seeing an enormous statue out in the water. I was only able to see the head and the long arm holding something up in the air.

When we got off the ship, I encountered strangers kissing me and passing me from one person to another. Here was a new set of relatives waiting for us. Strangers were telling me they were my

Nonno Nino and Nonna Giuseppa, Papa's father and mother, and a new set of aunts and uncles. Papa was one of twelve brothers and sisters.

I was happy to see Zia Maria and Zio (uncle) Tato and cousins: Nino, Giuseppe, Giuseppa, and Vito who had lived across the street from us in Carini. They had immigrated to America a few months earlier. Their younger brother Mark was born on the Sathunia. Photographers and newspaper reporters had met them when they arrived at the pier in New York City. The city lavished gifts and money to this poor immigrant family who already had four kids.

I later found my Italian cousins to be supportive, as we all headed off to school at P.S. 154 in Brooklyn. My first day of school is a painful memory and a lesson in the beauty of the differences of humankind.

I had not known or experienced snow. We all walked through a vacant parking lot. At first I enjoyed this new thrill, but eventually ending up in tears; as my feet got colder, my black-patent leather shoes were not adequate. A nurse at the school rubbed my feet until they warmed up and my tears dried. They had a pair of boots waiting for me for the walk home. Her kindness has never been forgotten.

I was brought to first grade. The teacher sat me in an empty seat in the back of the classroom next to a young girl. She shyly smiled and pushed her book between us in order to share. I stared at her in amazement. She had such beautiful dark skin and bright eyes. I wished I had been dark like her. I had never seen anything so beautiful before. I had accepted the differences without question or prejudice, but with love and acknowledgment. At an early age I learned that differences are beautiful for what they are.

My cousins, brother, sister, and I must have seemed like a little tribe and some of the kids did not take kindly to us. We got stones thrown at us on our way to school and heard words that we did not understand. Since we seemed different, because they did not understand us, they did not accept us. It did not take long for us to learn the English language. I do not recall struggling to learn. It seemed that one day we did not understand a word and the next we were speaking fluently.

One of the first things the school did was to change our names. I was no longer Giuseppa but became Josephine, later shortened to Josie. Antonio became Anthony, later shortened to Tony and Rosetta became Rosie. At the time, the belief was to immerse everyone into the American culture, but at home we only spoke Italian and had brought our Italian culture with us.

Only Italians came to visit Mama and Papa, and we would visit only Italians in Brooklyn and Coney Island. It seemed that not many of them ever learned to speak English but had adapted American words into the Italian language. Mama and Papa would eventually learn to speak broken English, which I had thought were Italian words. It was while I was speaking to my Italian cousins in Italy that I realized this, as they laughed at me while trying to explain the proper word in Italian, for what I had thought was Italian. It appeared that most Italian immigrants in Brooklyn had learned the same American lingo for saying certain American words. Examples of this are keaka, for cake, luneonee for Union Street, cheekena for chicken, and so on.

The place where Mama and Papa worked hired predominately Italians. Papa found work in the construction of buildings. Mama worked down the street from where we lived sewing piecework in a clothing factory. On the first floor was a delicatessen and above it was the garment factory. It was located on 17th Street, 7th Avenue in Brooklyn. The factory was an open spacious room filled with women, each bent over the sewing machine working as fast as they could. I could still see Mama and hear the roaring sound of those sewing machines. Her head was bent down, her foot moving the machine as fast as she could handle, while turning the material and sewing it into place. The work that the women did on the garment was broken down into piecework. One woman worked on the sleeves, while another on the collar and so on. As soon as one bundle was completed, there would be another waiting. Mama worked hard and tried to outdo the previous week in order to make more money.

Sunday afternoon's relatives would stop by and Papa would take out the gallon of wine that he had made. The kids and I would gather in the backyard and amuse ourselves playing while the women would gather in the kitchen.

A few incidents have remained with me from my early years in Brooklyn that had been etched in my young mind. I went to my first birthday party that first year in America, which I have never forgotten, not for what it was, but for the kindness of strangers. Judy was the young girl's name whose birthday party I attended. I do not recall any of the other students' names or what they looked like from my class but I will always remember Judy and her mother.

Judy was a little girl with blond hair and blue eyes. The mother came to the school and walked the class to her home. I must not have been properly dressed for a birthday party because Judy's mother took me up to her daughter's room and changed my clothes into one of her daughter's dresses. It was shear white with purple violets. After tying the bow on the dress, she gave me a wonderful warm smile and nudged me towards the bedroom door to join the party. I do not recall the party at all, only the wonderful gesture this kind woman showed me. Over the years, I have sent her a million bouquets of thanks for her kindness. She and Judy walked me home after the party.

Our first Christmas in America was memorable. A wonderful neighbor from across the street in Brooklyn brought gifts for us kids. We didn't know that people received gifts on Christmas. Our custom had been to place our shoes outside the front door on January 6 and Santa Befana would leave us candy. She was our Italian Saint Nicholas. The generous neighbor gave Rosetta, who was two years younger, a Barbie doll and I got paper dolls.

I wanted my sister's doll so badly. I had never had a doll and had amused myself for hours with the doll Mama created by tying together two dishtowels. My heart ached as my sister cut the dolls blond hair off. She soon tired of the doll and I lovingly rescued it and took over the care of that doll.

It would be the only doll I would ever have as a child. It only happened because of the thoughtfulness of the neighbor. She may have forgotten the kind gesture that she did but I have not forgotten. The small gifts that she gave have gone back to her with thankfulness, that I have sent her way over the years.

I was soon roller skating, riding my best friend Louise's bike, and singing American songs. I learned to play jump rope, jacks, old maid, knuckles, and handball. Like many American children, I too rushed home from school and watched the Mickey Mouse Club, the Three Stooges, Abbot and Costello and American Band Stand. I believe these show had been the best tools for my learning the English language.

In those early years in America, I received my first holy communion. My best friend Louise and I were walking to the movie theater, at the circle of Prospect Park, still dressed in my white communion dress. A stranger stopped us. He was tall, fair skinned, with the most wonderful warm blue eyes. He bent down, smiled, patted me on the head, and gave me a quarter. I can still see the stranger's face after all these years. I had a feeling that this was a special moment. I have often wondered over the years, why the stranger's face has stayed with me since the tender age of eight. Why was his face an imprint on my mind and soul? I now wondered, could he have been an angel?

Walking around Carini and recalling those memories, I had time to ponder many things. The face of two men unexpectedly emerged in my mind as one. The one who had given me the twenty-five cents as a child and years later, the man at the realty office, who had given me twenty dollars, I now understood was the same person. Their eyes, faces, smiles, posture, and demeanor was the same. To come to this conclusion came as a surprise to me. Each of them had left a familiar imprint on my mind. Now, at this moment in my life when I was the most vulnerable, the knowledge was linked. Could there be a reason for this knowledge connecting now, I wondered? If there was, what could it possibly be?

Here I was back in Italy, back in the country that gave me birth. I was home. My family was well known in Carini. Part of my family had stayed behind or returned from America to their beloved country. People recognized my family resemblance and would stop to speak with me about Papa, Mama, Zia and Zio in America, only they called me, Mericana, (the American.) Who was I? Was I Italian or American? Which country did I belong to? In America, I felt Italian and that others treated me that way and in Italy, they treated me as an American. I struggled to find my identity in so many ways. I was now questioning my rightful place in the world. It was as though neither country claimed me as theirs. Doesn't any country want me, I wondered.

There was an urgent need inside of me to visit my grandparents' grave before I left Carini. The graves in Italy are very different from the ones we have in America. They are above ground and family members will be stacked one on top of the other, with their individual pictures encased in glass on each drawer.

I searched for Nonno Giuseppe and Nonna Rosa. "I have to find them. I need to talk and connect with them." I ran up and down the aisles of the graveyard searching for the familiar photos with tears streaming down my face. There was an urgency and need to touch where their bodies were laid. I finally found them and recognized them. Their picture looked the same as when I had left them as a child.

I embraced the cold stone and took turns placing my face on the glass-enclosed pictures of my grandparents. I wailed with tears, "Help me. Give me the strength to go on living. You had to endure the pain of separation, in order to encourage your children to leave Italy for a better life. I am a product of your sacrifice. I cannot fail you by failing at life. I can't let you down. I need your strength."

My heart was breaking and tears would not subside, as I continued to press my face on the cold stone. Silence suddenly seemed to fill me. With clouded eyes, I looked intently at their familiar faces. I felt as though they had reached out from the other side and engulfed me with comfort, love, and peace. I was now ready to leave Italy.

On the long plane flight back to America I had time to reflect upon many things. I am no longer a wife but still a mother. Albert, Louise, and I are a family and I have to regroup. I am no longer the person that I was and I need to find who I am. Deciding to reclaim my maiden name was only the beginning of my search. I went back and forth, as to whether I was Italian or American.

I had not realized, at the time, that this was a turning point in my gaining strength. I had visited my roots and Italy had nourished me. This had given me a gentle touch and the nudge I needed to get back to life.

WE ARE ANSWERED IN VARIOUS WAYS

I sensed that I was coming back to America with a new found strength, which was needed, to reclaim my life. I was forced to accept the fact that I had to create a new direction to be able to support my children and myself. As our plane landed at Kennedy Airport, I came to the understanding that I was both Italian and American. Italy had given me birth and America had given me a new life; and now, I had the opportunity to do that again. I understood that I had the best of both worlds; I was part of both countries.

Changing back to Basile, my maiden name, was easy. I had kept it as my middle name during my marriage. I was able to change my last name by providing documentation to the Social Security Office and the Bureau of Licenses. I also had an urgency to change from Josie to Giuseppa. I wanted to be me, the whole me of who I was. I felt broken and had to start somewhere to put it back together. Being Josie had been a painful existence. Perhaps in some way I wanted to recapture the times of being innocent and being loved. Being Giuseppa was that time. My birth certificate was not enough documentation to prove that my real name was Giuseppa and so I stayed "Josie." In time, I would come to accept the fact that I was much more than just a name; after all, that is only a word, not the true essence of me.

I was fearful of the unknown. I did not know where I was going, nor did I know where to begin. I had lost control over the changes that happened in my life. It was difficult and painful to accept an unknown future. Even with all my spiritual experiences,

I did not have the foresight to know that this was a path that I was meant to be on. I only knew that I had two teenage children with nothing to fall back on to support us.

Over the years Mama and Papa had sold their restaurant Mama Nina's in Oneonta to my brother Frank. They started another restaurant across from their home in Stamford called Mama Maria's. Papa named it after Mama. I started working there as a server. To say that I felt lost is understating the reality of my life. I still questioned how God could allow this to happen to me. At times, I felt like a zombie, lost in thoughts. The pain in my heart felt as though a knife was stabbing it and would not let up.

I went to church one day and knelt in front of the statue of Mother Mary. I looked up at her and said, "You are supposed to be the mother of all people. You can't possibly be my mother; you would not have allowed this pain in my heart!" I said it with such conviction and belief.

That evening I had a dream in another reality. In my dream I walked into my Brother Frank's restaurant. It was very bright. After walking in I saw a small bag of clothes that I recognized as belonging to my cousin Rosa. I will bring it to her, I thought in my dream. As soon as I stepped outside, darkness consumed me. I was stuck and could not move backward or forward because there was no light to go by and the restaurant became dark and disappeared. I understood this was the condition of my life—I was stuck.

I was scared and yelled out, "Oh Blessed Mother, help me!" In the darkness, I heard a voice from above that spoke to me in Italian, "Giuseppa, it is me . . . your mother . . . I am here . . . You are my daughter . . . You are truly my daughter . . ."

The voice was beautiful and comforting. I was no longer scared. At that moment, I found myself in front of my home with all the lights on and it was very bright again. I walked into the house and woke up.

I went to the church the following morning and knelt in front of the statue of the Blessed Mother, humbled by what I had experienced. I said with passion, "Please forgive me for ever doubting you".

Shortly afterwards I realized that the stabbing pain in my heart had gone away. One moment it was there, and then it was gone. This amazed me at the way it had played out.

Of course, I still felt that I was the ultimate failure. For months, I kept thinking, "I am a failure. I failed at my marriage." I was so overcome with these thoughts and they constantly replayed in my mind. This feeling of failure was overwhelming, paralyzing me with emotions of defeat.

One day, at the grocery store, speaking low to a friend at the cashier station, I said, "I feel like a failure after twenty-one years of marriage."

A woman standing behind me tapped me on the shoulder and said, "Dear, you are not a failure. You had twenty-one years of success." I looked at her flabbergasted, but those words sank within me with such an impact.

This new thought penetrated me, "I am not a failure." These words gave me cause to pause and reflect. The mere fact that I had put up with so much abuse during the twenty-one years of marriage, was truly an achievement. I had stuck it out and put myself aside, in the hope that William's behavior would change. It wasn't me who had failed, but William. He was the one who walked away, not accepting his responsibility for his drinking, children, wife, or home. As long as I was taking the responsibility of our failed marriage, I was still defending him and taking ownership for his actions; and therefore, stuck in my life. This was certainly a different perspective.

How the woman ever heard me talking with my friend I will never know. She was a stranger; yet, those words stayed with me. There was a mysterious feeling to that encounter. Could she have been an angel who helped me see the failed marriage in a different perspective, I wondered?

I don't remember the friend I was speaking with but have never forgotten the stranger's kind words of comfort, understanding, and liberation. Shortly after that incident, I realized that the heaviness of guilt and the feeling of failure had vanished.

At one point Papa said, "You have to take whatever life gives you, and make the best of it." Papa's words awakened a feeling of direction. Those words lingered within me. He was right. I had to accept what was before me. Accept the now, I thought.

I realized that struggling, rejecting, refusing, and resisting my present life made it harder and more painful to move forward. I could not turn back the clock, nor could I accept the way it had been. I have to take steps to move forward because there is no return to the past. This was a different way of seeing what had been and a new way of seeing what was now.

My friend Angie, a real estate broker, would say to me, "People come into one's life for a reason, a season, or a lifetime." William had many fine qualities that I had admired and loved, but they were never continuous, just bits and pieces thrown at me here and there. What I had to accept was the fact that William's season and reason had come and gone.

Eventually I would understand that the time had come for William to get off the stage of my life. New players were waiting in the wings and they could not enter until William left the stage of act one. There was much preparation behind the scenes of my life, which I was not aware of at the time. How could I have imagined that I had wondrous new acts ahead of me?

"Perhaps," I said to Mama one day, "The gift was that William left us. Louise, Albert, and I deserve a better life than dealing with an alcoholic father and husband for the rest of our lives."

How could I have known that this was only part of the gift and that there was much more, which was unfolding on its own time. I had no idea that the transformation had just begun.

FINDING MY VOICE

My voice within and my identity were in crisis. I was struggling in search for both. Guiding my children into adulthood was left on my shoulders. It was a heavy burden. William had just walked away and never looked back. There was no one to lean on to help me. "Wait till your father gets home," had been powerful words. I had lost so much in so many different ways.

I was hanging on and trying to control what was left in my life, Louise and Albert. There was an underlying fear of losing them too. I had lost sight of the fact that they were teenagers struggling with their own identities, as well as the upheaval in our lives.

The three of us were in the midst of constant battles. This compounded the pain and struggles we were experiencing. I was holding on tightly while they wanted to explore their boundaries. The dynamics of our scattered family unit was straining with pain in every dimension. Everything in our life had changed all at once, especially in mine.

One day I was reprimanding Louise for having a messy room. She looked at me straight in the eye and said, "Mom, I am a good kid. I get good grades. I don't do drugs. I am home when I am expected. Pick your battles."

I looked at her astounded as the realization of her words, full of knowledge, penetrated me like a thunderbolt. She was right. I had to choose what was important and let go of unnecessary arguments or aspects of our lives that were no long relevant. I had to stop resisting the change in my children and accept their new stage of life, as well as my own.

This was a powerful lesson and it opened volumes to the many difficult situations we were now facing. This was a penetrating feeling of knowledge and understanding of truth, in all its raw essence. Acknowledging non-resistance and accepting the now, was as though another veil had been removed from my eyes. As soon as I stopped resisting the change, the struggles seemed to lessen. I was walking a tight rope and having a hard time in being in a non-resistant state. I kept the lines of communication open with my children. I accepted them for the individual strengths they each had. Allowing them the freedom to fall, they learned how to fly. In time, my reward would be the incredible adults they would become.

William had been the decision maker in our home. I had a say, but it was done in conjunction with him. My life had been consumed with trying to keep William sober, waiting and wondering when his next drinking binge would be. I had lost sight of my individuality and the person that had been me. I had become William's warden! He had to escape me in order for him to grow and take over responsibilities for his own life and actions. William's drinking was no longer my responsibility. The time had come for me to look at myself and reclaim my life. I had to take over the reins and I did not know where to begin.

The driveway at the house had always been dangerous. Albert was driving and Louise would be driving soon. Water ran down the middle of the driveway and this became a sheet of ice in the winter. It was steep and long. We had to take a head start from the main road and drive up fast in order to reach the top. To make it even worse, we then had to make a quick left turn at the top and head towards the garage. If the start was not fast enough, we would slide backwards, into the main road, and have to start all over again. This was dangerous, to say the least.

I decided to change the direction and location of the driveway. I believed the new location would be shorter, straight into the garage, without such an incline. I discussed the change of location with the two men in my life, Papa and Albert. Both of them disagreed with the decision that I wanted to make and both felt that the driveway would be worse.

I pondered for weeks about how they felt. I had to decide whether I should listen to them or to listen to this inner voice in me, "Change the driveway, you are right." I must have walked that lawn a million times, visualizing where the new driveway would be. Trying to make the decision consumed me. I decided to go against their opinion and stood by my choice. This was painful, but I felt that I had to take the chance that it would be safer.

I had the old driveway filled in. A shorter and straight driveway was created further up the road and had a straight drive into the garage. It did have less of an incline and the water did flow down the side, as I had hoped. Papa and Albert, eventually, had to admit that I had been right.

It was not just about making the driveway safer, or that I had been right that was important, but that I had made a decision on my own and had found my voice. For twenty-one years, I had been silenced in making any decision on my own. Making this choice gave me a new sense of strength and confidence that was needed to create my new path and new direction in life. This was the beginning of regaining my power, which I had given away.

How ironic: I opened a new path to the house as I was creating a new path in my life. *Remember the driveway*, became my mantra when I had to make a decision. From that time on, I listened to what others had to say, but I would make the final choice because my mantra would suddenly replay in my head.

I had no idea where I was going with my life; yet, there was an expectation inside of me of waiting. I started getting this burst of internal joy and didn't know what it was, or understand the reason why this bleep of excitement should happen. There was no way of my knowing that my life was unfolding according to plan. My life was being transformed, one-step at a time. I was on a path and journey from which there would be no return.

On weekends, I continued to work in Mama and Papa's restaurant, and during the week, in the real estate office. I knew that neither job was stable. I had to find job stability to support my children. My future was still a dilemma.

One day, I was in the kitchen, ironing clothes, going over the condition of my life. Talking to God but mostly to myself, I inwardly said, "God help me. What am I going to do with my life?" It was said in such humbleness, wonderment, and questioning. I really did not expect an answer.

A commercial came on television showing adult women going back to college and obtaining college degrees in order to better their lives. Okay, I can do that, I thought. Until I know what to do, I will go to college and take some courses.

Could it be that I had asked for direction and it presented itself to me in the form of a commercial? I did not realize, at the time, that I had never seen that commercial before, nor have I seen it since. What are the odds that the situation just seemed to resolve itself as soon as I had asked for help, with passion and belief from within?

This was another life altering experience, which opened a new direction and path. How could I have known that the journey was unfolding according to plan.

I called up the college and set an appointment. That fall, 1994, I became a full-time college student at the State University of New York at Oneonta, which is in my hometown. I could not think about the many college years ahead of me, but chose to concentrate on one semester at a time. I struggled and worked hard. I was so afraid of failure. I was so vulnerable and weak inside. I had to give up my job in real estate but continued to work on the weekends in the restaurant.

Many times, I would ask myself, what am I doing in college? I was lost in so many ways. People do this sort of thing when they are young, not at my age.

Nothing could have prepared me for the ultimate spiritual experiences that were yet to come.

ULTIMATE GIFT

There seemed to be an anticipation and extreme excitement inside of me as 1995 was coming to a close and 1996 was beginning. I felt that something significant was going to happen. I could not understand what it could possibly be.

Every so often, I would feel a burst of incredible joy within. The feeling was a jolt of immense bliss and then, just as quickly, passed. As the New Year got closer, I experienced the jolts of joy more often, deeper, and more intensely. A thought would always enter at those times and it replayed repeatedly, "Something wonderful is going to happen to me this year, but what?"

This was my third year of college. I was starting to enjoy the taste of this new freedom, that I deserved a good life and a wonderful future.

The spring of that year, I became active in the Non-Traditional Student Organization, and I was elected president. I was holding what was to be my first meeting, and little did I know, my last, because of events that were about to unfold. The meeting was held in the coffee shop where most college professors and some students congregated for lunch. This was unusual, as we had never held a meeting there before. I don't know why I had chosen to hold my first meeting there.

I arrived early for the meeting and noticed two college professors that I knew, one from a class I had taken and one from a class I wanted to take. I went over to speak to them. Professor Walter VanSaul, an education instructor whom I knew from the previous class was with Professor Ashok Malhotra, a philosophy professor. When I saw Professor Ashok, I remembered about the class I had wanted to take from him.

"Professor Ashok," I said, "I was going to enroll in your Buddhism class for next fall and noticed that is not being offered."

"I am taking a group of students to study abroad in India," he said. "Why don't you join us and study Buddhism there?"

"Are you going to the Taj Mahal?"

"Well yes, and many other temples as well."

"I have always wanted to visit the Taj Mahal."

"Then you should come," he stated.

"I can't go to India. I have children, a house, and bills to pay."

Professor Ashok stopped by our table on his way out the door and said, "You know, you really should think about coming to India."

"Yea, yea," I said wistfully, "Thank you, but there is no way that I can possibly go to India."

Visiting the church, when no one was there, had become a ritual with me. As I was walking out of the church that Friday, I ran into Father Roman on the front steps of the church. We stopped to chat.

"When are you coming to see me to have your marriage annulled?" he asked.

"Father," I said, "how can my marriage be annulled? I have two children."

"It's not exactly that way," he replied. "I have not seen you in church lately."

"I am not sure what my beliefs are; besides, I have not been to confession in a long time, Father."

"Well," he said, "that should not stop you from coming to church." Somehow, we decided that I would confess my sins to him right there on the church steps. He absolved me of my sins. It never occurred to me that this was an unusual thing we were doing. I suppose there is no need to be inside the church to have this interaction with the priest. It would be years later until I realized it was purification that was needed in order to proceed to the next level of my spiritual growth.

A friend, Elizabeth Koenig, called me that evening and invited me to attend a seminar in Albany for the following day. Elizabeth is tall and slender with exotic features. She had been supportive when I returned to college. Her daughter Mary and my daughter Louise were best friends since nursery school. Considering I had to waitress by three o'clock on the afternoon of the seminar, I did not want to go for fear that I would be late. However, for some reason, I was compelled to go. This event would become the pinnacle and turning point in my life, from which a new journey would begin. Everything in my life had happened to lead me to this moment.

The seminar was on 'The Fourth Dimension' presented by Henry Bolduc and Henry Reed from the Edgar Casey Institute. I recall that the topic involved the belief that we all have the potential to tap into the source of knowledge. I was at a loss.

They handed out paper and asked us to write or draw the first thing that came to our minds. For no apparent reason I drew a triangle with an eye in the middle and lines for energy emanating from the triangle.

A woman sitting next to me leaned over and said, "That's interesting."

"It is?" I did not know what it was or why I drew that symbol. I have since come to understand that it is the third eye, which we all have, of inner knowledge. It is also considered the symbol of God's mastery of the universe, the all-seeing and all-knowing eye.

We were then encouraged to close our eyes and go with the flow of what we were experiencing. I could hear around me the scraping of chairs, heavy breathing, and people coughing. With my eyes closed I found myself looking up towards a bright light at the end of what appeared to be a tunnel. Before me appeared two figures in brown robes. I understood they were angels and were there to escort me.

With the two angels on each side of me, I felt as though I was floating up towards the light, as it got bigger and brighter. I was amazed at what I was experiencing and had a deep desire to understand. I kept thinking over and over, "This can't be happening," and at the same time believing the experience.

I found myself in front of a radiant light and knew it was God. It was as though the light was continuously growing and emitting love. There was no booming voice, as one would hear in a Charlton Heston movie, but there was acceptance that this was God—limitless love. The light was warm and comforting on my face and in my whole being. I ached for more of that immense feeling. I heard myself inwardly ask, "Please God, let me feel your . . . ."

Before I had finished the thought, a piece of the light separated and came towards me like a slow arrow, filling my body and soul with love and joy beyond human words. This was the same burst and jolt of joy that I had experienced, except now it was intense, constant, and deep within the essence of my being. I bathed in the majestic magnitude of the incredible bliss of joy and love. There was an abandonment of restrictions, being at one with God and humanity. It was a familiar feeling that I first experienced in the dream reality with Katherine.

Tears of joy flowed down my cheeks. I tried to raise my hand to wipe the tears but my arm would not rise and I realized that my tears were dry. I understood my body was sitting in the room but my spirit, my soul, the essence of me, had transcended into another reality, only this time, not in a dream.

I was experiencing the essence of love in Truth form. The words God, Divine, and all the words that God is called, seemed so diminutive compared to what I was experiencing. "I am that I am," seemed to echo within me. I was connecting with the source, the light, the giver of life, Love, Truth, and it was spiritual, magical, and immense. God had touched me!

Mere mortal words cannot express the essence of the love that was within me. Nirvana was the state of my existence. It was a release of boundaries, a feeling of limitless love, and an understanding of all knowledge. There was a communion in the connection, beyond explanation. It was humbling, but I had acceptance of being in my rightful place.

I found myself looking out into void, a vastness of nothingness; and yet, there was sacredness in the essence of nothingness. There was stillness within and without. I was aware of the awareness and volumes of knowledge were understood in the quietness of the nothingness. There was a connection within the depth of my soul to the vastness and greatness of the nothingness; the essence of God was in the nothingness and vastness of quietness, which is in everything. I was in total immersion with the universe and with the essence of the Divine. No human words can explain this profound and humbling wonder. I had reached beyond the physical plane of life and past the illusion of the reality in which I lived. I knew these things with total acceptance and conviction.

I experienced the greatness of the Divine and this can only be understood in spirit form. I looked out into the void of the creation. I accepted the remembrance of the nothingness and the void. We are all an aspect of the Divine, in the I am that I am, which is in all, and is part of All.

I knew all the answers to the universe and felt oneness with humankind and with All that Is. I saw humanity interconnected like a web. What one human spirit does to another, affects us all. The words of me and we, are one and the same. The source of Love does not see us separately but as an expression of His infinite love.

There are no sins that the All that Is has not forgiven before they even happen. He loves us all equally and unconditionally, the sinner as well as the saint. The Divine acknowledges all religions and all are seen as one, and none above or better than the other, regardless of the differences in their teachings.

There was much more that I understood in that manifestation but was not able to process or bring back with me because I have human limitations and comprehension. Eventually, more understanding would filter-in slowly over the years, in the Divine's timing.

Then I was back and I could hear Elizabeth calling, "Josie— Josie". I felt as though I was being pulled back. I was lightheaded and dazed, my face hot. I opened my eyes. I was overwhelmed with the experience I had in another reality, and the realization that it had not happened in a dream. I was weak and numb. My energy was slowly coming back.

I could not believe what I had just experienced. The feeling of the incredible joy and love was still vibrating in every fiber of my being. The feeling was of confusion and a deep desire to maintain that love inside. However, I could feel it already ebbing from when I first experienced it.

I glanced up at Elizabeth. She was looking at me intently with a bewildered look in her eyes. "What happened," she asked. I could not speak; I could only stare at her in wonderment with both belief and disbelief. She knew something had happened and exclaimed, "Nothing ever happens to me."

There was still more to come that would be connected to that day and week.

At the seminar, that afternoon, we were asked to pair up with another individual. Standing alone I saw another woman on the other side of the room, also standing. We looked at each other and motioned for us to sit together during the next exercise. We introduced ourselves, her name was Joan. We did not have time to say anything else because instructions were being given.

We were to sit facing each other with our eyes closed to wait for answers from the other side. I closed my eyes and what flashed before me was a crown of thorns on a heart. I then saw Jesus walking in the sand carrying Joan in His arms. These things were very vivid, and I felt the experience was actually happening as I visualized this encounter.

"What did you see?" she asked excitedly. I could not answer her. How could I tell her that I understood horrible pain was coming into her life? I hesitated.

"All right," she said, "I will go first."

She was jubilant and said, "I saw you going to another world. You will be traveling. You will be making speeches. Your work will be known all over the world. You will be traveling over water but to another world." She was puzzled as to another world and could not explain the meaning.

None of what she said made sense to me. "Joan," I said, "I hear what you are saying but somehow it seems impossible. I rarely venture out on my own, and usually when I do, not much further than an hour away from home alone. Giving speeches? I am scared to death to speak in front of crowds."

"I can't explain it but I saw these things very clearly about you. I don't understand about another world but that is what I saw," Joan said.

Incredulous as it may seem, I did not even think about the morning experience. I have come to understand that my spiritual experiences don't interplay but will eventually connect. It's as though previous experiences have to take a step back for the new experiences to come forward. One spiritual experience after another would have been a bombardment to the humaneness in me. This would have made me incapable of processing the authenticity of the present experience.

"Ok, what did you see? Your turn," she excitedly said. I stumbled, stuttered and nothing came out. "You have to tell me," she begged.

I blurted out, "Joan, there is pain coming into your life. I saw a crown of thorns on your heart. You will not be alone; Jesus will carry you through this." I could not believe what I was saying to this poor woman.

She sat back in her chair and did not say a word. She looked at me with sadness in her eyes. I was horrified at what I had said.

"Perhaps none of this is true, Joan. What you said to me seems impossible; perhaps, what I am telling you is wrong." Somehow the sadness in her eyes told me that she did believe what I had said. We exchanged phone numbers. I had no idea why we did that.

Six months later I called Joan, and we shared our experiences of the past six months. I was amazed with the information we shared.

"Josie, I could not believe what you said to me that day in Albany. My daughter had been diagnosed with an incurable disease, bleeding from every orifice of her body. I had accepted that fact when I came to the seminar. I was also handling the fact that my husband had left us and I had to learn how to drive so I could go to college. What I had not expected was my beloved nephew would be diagnosed with an incurable cancer, and would die in my arms. The pain had been so overwhelming that God had to have carried me to get me through."

What I had seen, unfortunately, had happened . . .extreme pain of human endurance. Her prediction of my experiences would also unfold in the most incredulous way.

I had to leave the seminar early or would be late for work. It was raining so hard that there were large puddles of water on the road. My car hydroplaned going around a curve on the highway. By all accounts I should have crashed that day. My car seemed to have wings and it flew around the long, treacherous curve, as if it was being lifted and carried to safety.

I worked that evening but I kept going over in my mind

the events of that day. The feeling of intense love, which had permeated my body that day, was dissipating slowly. I could not believe what happened. I have no idea how I got through the night. Well nothing can top this experience, I thought. How wrong could I be!

GOD YOU CAN'T POSSIBLY MEAN ME

There was still a residue of that love inside me, the following Wednesday, as I went to church for the celebration of Father Roman's twenty-fifth anniversary of being a priest. As I walked into the church, I saw Mama and my sister-in-law Mariana sitting in the front pew. They had saved me a seat. The church was packed with people of the community from various faiths, churches, and temples. There were dignitaries from the Albany diocese.

The mass proceeded as usual. Guest speakers were presented. A representative read a speech from Bishop Hubbard of Albany.

Suddenly everything went quiet within me. I heard a gentle, comforting voice in my left ear and felt the breath, *"Feed my lambs."*

I turned towards where the voice was coming from and answered back in my head, "You mean sheep, don't you Lord?"

The gentle voice repeated, *"Feed my lambs."*

God is talking to me? I thought. Who am I that God should speak to me? I was stunned.

Nothing else existed, only the voice, the questions, and the responses I was about to hear.

A speaker came up to the podium and said, *"Every day God chooses ordinary people to do His work."*

"God you want me to do something for you? You mean me? How can I possibly do something for you? How would I know what to do, what to say?"

The second speaker came up to the podium and said, *"God*

will put the words in your mouth and the people in your path who will help you."

I was feeling numb by this time. I was dazed. I could not believe what I was hearing. I was having a conversation with God and he was asking me to do something for Him. "Lord, what if I fail?" I inwardly asked.

The third guest speaker came up to the podium and said, *"You cannot fail, it is God's plan, not yours."*

"God no—Go to someone else, please. No God, no, please! Whatever it is you want me to do I cannot do it," I begged.

The next speaker came up to the podium and said, *"When God calls—you answer. He will put a burning desire in your heart that you cannot help but follow."*

I was compelled to give in. I surrendered for the moment. "Okay, under one condition. No pain!" God must have a sense of humor to come to me, I thought. Then I inwardly begged, "I don't want to change the person that I am Lord. I don't want to become one of those holier than thou people. I still want to be me."

I don't know what I was thinking. Couldn't I have asked for a million dollars? No pain and don't change me were the best I could think of.

At the reception for Father Roman, I wandered around lost in my thoughts, going over what I had just experienced. I had no idea what it all meant or what I was supposed to do.

My daughter's high school teacher and his wife came up to me and asked, "Where is Louise going to college this fall?"

I answered them without my knowledge of what I was saying until I said it, "She is going to Albany University and I hope you will visit her because I am going to India".

It's a good thing there was a seat next to me because I plopped down into it. I was stunned and shocked. I panicked. "India? Where did that come from? You want me to go to India, Lord? Where is India?"

Last Wednesday I had heard about the India trip from

Professor Ashok but had not thought about it since and here it was out of my mouth, saying, "I am going to India." I was dazed and shocked, to say the least.

I tossed and turned all night. "God you made a mistake. You can't possibly mean me go to India. I don't want to go to India." I was overwhelmed with fear at the prospect of going to India. This was a new concept that I was not ready to handle or even remotely interested in doing. I had made a commitment to God and had accepted without knowing what it was He wanted me to do.

I had to connect to someone. I went to church the following morning and found Father Roman on the altar directing people in the breakdown of the extra chairs from the previous evening's event. I walked up to the altar. Looking up at Father Roman I barely whispered, "Father, need to speak to you." I was not able to sit where I had sat the previous evening. I sat a few pews away and stared at the spot in disbelief and wonder. I was still stunned, at what had happened when I had sat there. Father Roman came over and sat next to me.

"What is it Josie?" Father asked.

"He spoke to me last night."

Father Roman bent forward and curiously asked, "Whom?"

"God!"

"What did He say?"

"Feed my Lambs."

Father Roman gasped, "Do you know what the scripture was this morning?"

"No!" Nor did I care at that moment.

"It was about feeding God's Lambs." We both sat there in silence. After a moment he said, "God has touched you. It will be interesting to see how far this will go."

This was not what I wanted to hear. I wanted him to say it was impossible; I must have imagined it; anything but what he said. I walked out of the church more confused. I was lost in thoughts of fear and wonder that day. The fact that God had spoken to me seemed irrelevant at this point. I did not know what to do with this new revelation that God was asking of me.

I did not understand at the time, nor did I wonder what God meant by feeding his lambs. It would be years later that the understanding came to me: God wanted me to feed His children. The people on earth are considered the lambs of God and God is the Shepherd.

Thursday night in bed I tossed, turned, cried, and begged, "God, please go to someone else. You must be making a mistake coming to me. I am nobody Lord." I now tried to reason with God. "What if I die Lord? There are so many diseases in India. Who will take care of my children?" I was a child before him, with all the vulnerabilities of being human.

Then something mysterious happened by my bedroom window. A shadow of a person appeared. I could make out a veil and robe.

She said, "Be not afraid. I will be with you every step of the way while you are in India." She said it in such a comforting and reassuring voice. Even though I could not see the face I inwardly acknowledged who she was. It was Saint Theresa.

I had not known much about Saint Theresa. It would be years later that I learned; Saint Theresa is the patron saint of India and the guardian of missions.

The struggles vanished after I heard those words. I had run out of arguments. I gave in and accepted the fact that I was going to India. "God you want me to go to India . . . okay . . .What am I supposed to do there?" I fell into a deep and comforting sleep.

The next morning I awoke feeling refreshed but anxious. I had to go to the International Office and sign up for the trip. I went to my first period class, Statistics. I spotted Jane, another non-traditional student, in our usual front seat. We would sit there together with eager looks on our faces and blank expressions in our eyes as we tried to understand Statistics. She and I had a bond; we both hated the subject.

As I slipped into a seat next to her I whispered, "Jane, I have to go to the International Office to sign up to go to India."

"And so you shall," she said with such authority that I was stunned at her reaction.

I had hoped she would say, "Are you crazy? Why?" Some kind of argument would have felt great and perhaps would have become an out for me. Jane was the only person I had spoken to concerning the decision I was making. She was not cooperating by discouraging me as I had hoped she would.

When we arrived at the International Office, I could not fill out the forms. Fear gripped me. My hand trembled and I was baffled at what I was about to do. Jane filled out the forms for me and I signed them. I felt relief from the fear and confusion, for a brief moment after signing.

By afternoon, the reality of the commitment I had made was starting to sink in. I had signed up to do a three-month semester abroad, in a country I knew nothing about, with young students from various parts of the United States.

The thought had not occurred to me that going to India could place me behind in credit hours and then not be able to graduate next spring. Nor did I think of the responsibilities of how I was going to pay for the trip, the house bills, mortgage, insurance and other responsibilities. It was as though my mind had gone blank from any rational thinking before I signed the papers. Apparently, I was not meant to think of those things at the time. I can't even imagine the stress that those thoughts would have created. Miraculously, everything worked out.

CHILDREN'S INDIA FUND

The first problem I had to face was how do I tell Mama, Papa, and my children that I was going to India? What kind of explanation could I possibly give them? How would they react? I had to do it. *'Remember the driveway,'* I thought.

I walked into the restaurant one day and informed Mama and Papa, "I am going to India and don't try to stop me." I don't know where that forcefulness came from. Mama and Papa did not say a word. They stopped in their tracks, stood there, looked at me in shock and then continued with their work. Mama later informed me that something prevented her from voicing her fear about my going to India.

Telling my children was even harder. How could there be a right moment? They were still working through the loss of their father in their life. I had no choice and knew I had to tell them about what already had been set in motion. I sat them both on the couch one day, facing them and said, "I have something to tell you both. I am doing a semester abroad and I am going to India." At first they stared at me. I watched their faces, as the reality of what I was saying sunk in their minds.

"Mom, you can't go to India. I'm going to college. I need you here," wailed Louise.

"Who is going to take care of us?" Albert asked.

"Everything is going to be fine. I have to do this."

Louise lashed out at me, "You are being selfish! How can you leave us?"

"Louise, you are going to college and won't be here. You'll

be busy with school and making new friends. Your father lives in Albany, near the University. Albert, you are working at Uncle Frank's restaurant. You are always busy and rarely home."

"We need you here Mom," Louise stated angrily as she stormed out of the room.

God help me, I inwardly begged. Guide me to help my children cope with this. Albert sat there and looked stunned at this new revelation that I had thrust upon them. I was weakening, having felt their pain. I begged God to give me the strength to deal with the turmoil I had created in my children's lives. I had expected some resistance but had not expected this much pain and anger. My heart was crying at their anguish in knowing that they had the feeling of abandonment, yet again in their lives. I could not relent to their demands and could not explain the reason why I was taking such a stance. "God, you have got to take care of my children. I am going to India for you. This is not negotiable."

The following weeks I pondered the reasons for going to India. How will I know what it is I am supposed to do? Professor Ashok was away on retreat completing a book with Professor Doug and would not return to the area for two weeks.

When Professor Ashok returned my phone call, I had a burning question in my heart that I needed an answer to. "Tell me about the children in India."

He said, "Well they have families and . . ."

"No," I interrupted. "Are they poor?"

"Well, yes," he said.

"Then, I will raise money for the children before we leave for India."

A meeting was set up to meet with Professor Suzanne and Professor Ashok to discuss my plan. "The children in India are poor so I will raise money to perhaps do something for them. I will call it, The Children's India Fund." Where this was coming from I had no idea. Words were coming out of my mouth and my thinking was being confirmed by the words I was saying. My rationality was, "I still don't know why I am going to India so, by having money available, I will be able to help the children, until I know the reason why I am going." How could I possibly have known, that it was exactly what I was supposed to be doing.

Professor Ashok turned to Professor Suzanne and said, "This is perfect, falls right in with the 'Learn and Serve' concept of this trip. The students will take classes and will also be doing community charity work. Perhaps we can use the money to help with the various projects that the students will be working on."

Years later, I learned that Professor Ashok had not organized a trip to India in years. At the last moment that semester, he decided to put the program together. He had not expected enough students to sign up, since the information was posted late in the semester. He also invited for the first time, an education instructor, Professor Suzanne to join the trip. He changed the concept from previous years of just studying abroad and added a new component of community service. He named the trip, 'Learn and Serve.' The progression of events was not complete until I became the final player. Years later I learned that Professor Ashok had not done a trip in years. At the last moment he decided to put the program together. He had not expected enough students would sign up since the information was out late in the semester. He also invited, for the first time an education instructor, Professor Suzanne, to join him on the trip. He changed the concept of previous years of just studying and called it, 'Learn and Serve.' The sequence of events had been in place, before I became the final player, that came on stage in the drama that was unfolding before us.

The first individual with whom I discussed why I was going to India was my cousin Rosa Brindle. I said, "I know this sounds crazy but this is what happened." I told her of the experiences that had occurred a few weeks earlier. I explained how in one week's time my life had completely changed by the sequence of events.

Rosa immediately came on board. She never had any question

or doubt of raising money for the children of India. She was creative and full of ideas.

"How are we going to get the word out about The Children's India Fund?" I asked her.

"I have an idea," Rosa said, "The Memorial Day Parade is coming up. How about getting tee shirts and have children's handprints on them. I will ask some of my women friends from the church and their children to wear them in the parade. The mothers can walk with their children or the children can be in strollers. I will make a banner with the Children's India Logo on it. Two children will carry the banner in the parade. The children can carry balloons, or they can be tied to the strollers." Rosa amazed me with her dedication. I was still scared and confused. Rosa was a tower of strength. Her belief in what we had to accomplish held me up. She had a burning desire in her heart and she was relentless.

Her children, Patrick and Tommy, got to the point where they would run away from her when they saw her coming with a tee shirt. Their poor little hands were used for the handprints. The newspaper picked up on the story. The radio interviewed me about the raising of money for the children of India.

We bought more tee shirts. Rosa drew two Indian children holding hands with the logo 'I gave in 1996' and we had them professionally printed. We sold batches of them to local restaurants to sell to the community. Members of our families bought most of the tee shirts, since most of them own Italian restaurants in the area.

We asked various restaurants and hair salons to offer gift certificates for raffling. We made up flyers and many of the area churches allowed us to place them in their church bulletins. Mama and Papa offered their restaurant on the day it was closed, Mondays, for two hours to raise money for the fund. Papa prepared the meatballs, the sauce, and spaghetti for us to sell. Michelle, another waitress, took over the kitchen and I served the food. People from the Stamford area heard about the fund and supported generously. I spoke at the Kiwanis club of Stamford and they were generous with their donation. The money was adding up. Rosa and I had become consumed with what we had to do. Ideas about raising money took over our lives.

During this time, the group of college students who had enrolled for the semester abroad came together for a week of seminar at the college. This was in preparation for our trip to India. We were from various parts of the country and from different universities. We began with thirteen people, but in the end, only twelve would go.

Rosa and I wanted to enlist the college students to take part in the raising of funds. I discussed with them my plan for raising money for the children of India. Rosa gave strategies and information on how to raise the money. They agreed to go back to their respective areas and raise $1,000 each. I informed them that Rosa and I would raise $5,000. The students did not have the burning desire that Rosa and I had. They did not raise any money, because it was not their mission, it was ours.

By the middle of August, Rosa and I had raised $4,500. This in itself was miraculous. We live in a very small community and to raise that amount of money in such a short time was unbelievable, to say the least.

"This is going to be a lot of money in India. This will help many children," Professor Ashok said. I was elated!

I still was not sure if raising money was what I was supposed to be doing. I pondered every day, "Is this it, God? Is this what I am supposed to be doing, raising money?" No answers ever came, just a burning desire in my heart that I had to keep going.

I was able to obtain a larger school loan to cover my expenses at home and for the trip. I called William and asked him to stay in touch with his daughter. My family offered to stay in touch with her and assured me that if she needed anything they would be there for her. I knew that Albert would be in constant contact with his sister. I didn't have concerns about Albert. He was working with family in the restaurant.

I left for India with a belief that everything would be taken care of.

Katherine Marshall (2/25/1925—
10/22/1971), my spirit guide.

Nonna Rosa & Nonno
Guiseppe Ruffino on
their wedding day.

Amelia & me on First
Communion Day.

Cemetery where my
grandparents are buried
in Carini, Italy.

Mama's Passport, with Rosa, me & Antonio.

Memorial Day Parade in Oneonta, NY.

My fellow travelers & me at SUNY Oneonta before the trip.

Section 2

THE POOR DO NOT NEED OUR
SYMPATHY AND OUR PITY.

THE POOR NEED OUR LOVE
AND COMPASSION.

Mother Teresa

ANOTHER WORLD

Louise left for SUNY Albany the week before I left for India. She was still angry with me. I knew this was a difficult time for her. "I will only be gone for three months," I reassured her. "I will be back by Thanksgiving." Nothing I said seemed to comfort Louise and rightfully so. She isolated me. I could not reason with her nor did she want to listen to what I struggled to understand myself. I could not put in simple words the burning desire I had in my heart, concerning the fact that I had to do this.

How could I explain when I was still questioning what I had experienced? I was going to another part of the world that I knew nothing about. I had a mission to accomplish and I did not know what it was. "Am I doing the right thing, Lord? Look what has happened to my children." Their anguish tormented me; and yet, the desire to go was far greater.

Albert would become supportive. "If this is what you want to do Mom, then go ahead and do it." Albert and Rosa were there to see me off. They were excited as I left for the airport on September 10, 1996. I had no idea why God had chosen me to go to India. It was with blind faith and a belief that God would show me what He wanted to be accomplished.

The students who were enrolled for the fall semester in India were: Heather Mason and Patrick Hickey from SUNY Binghamton; Jennifer Borst and John Wickett from SUNY Fredonia; Esmahan Zuccar from SUNY Plattsburg; Bipina Patel from SUNY Albany; Amber Rehling from San Francisco State University; Maegan Lee, Luke Mahoney, Aaron Hunter and I from SUNY Oneonta. The students, the professors, Ashok Malhotra and Suzanne Miller, united at a designated location at Kennedy airport to leave on our flight to India. Each of us arrived at different intervals from various parts of the country. We were all excited to see one another and had much anticipation about the adventure we were about to embark upon, each of us with our own expectations and reasons.

As our plane was taxiing into New Delhi International Airport, my first thought was, "I am home." I had no idea why or where that came from. I could not wait to get off the plane. My jubilance was about to take a dive.

The New Delhi airport was quiet, dark, dirty, and had no resemblance to any airport I had ever seen. Outside were barefoot beggars sleeping on the dirty airport steps. The air hit me like a wave pounding the shore. There was a stifling heat with an unusual and unfamiliar pungent odor. It seemed as though I had walked into a black and white film, which took me to one hundred years earlier in time, and into another world. I was experiencing an awakening of all my senses and it was overwhelming. My reaction to what I was seeing and feeling was, "Oh my God, what have you gotten me into?"

We eagerly got into the waiting bus, which was taking us to a hotel in New Delhi. The group became subdued as we took in the sights from our air-conditioned bus.

The streets of New Delhi were crowded with barefoot people in filthy conditions. There were yelling vendors in the streets, selling their wares, on dilapidated carts. Men were dressed with material that was wrapped around their bodies called Dhoti. There were three-wheeled motorcars everywhere used for transportation. Their buses went by us, over-packed with people. There was a wall of men with their backs to us, which we later found out was a large public urinal. There were few women walking in the streets, their faces totally covered with veils except their darting penetrating eyes. Dirty barefoot children were everywhere, wandering around and begging for food and money. There were people sleeping in corners or on makeshift cots. I was overwhelmed to take all this in at once. The sights, the sounds, and the unfamiliar odors were swarming my mind into shock.

We stayed in New Delhi overnight and the next day we traveled by train to Varanasi. Some of the enthusiasm seemed to have returned to the group in the light of dawn. Thousands and thousands of people were at the train station. The noise was deafening with the sounds of unfamiliar languages.

The train expedition was an intense experience. Our group had overnight private compartments, away from the open section of where most of the people rode.

I walked through the train and saw people everywhere, squatting or lying down. The compartments were packed with people compressed together on the floor. People were holding on to goats and in the hot open compartment, there were filled milk cans. There were live chickens running around in the cooking section.

The women wore bright colors of pink, red, and blue saris. They covered their faces with veils when they saw me, except for their piercing eyes, filled with surprise and questioning. "Who are you? What are you doing here? This is our compartment, go back to where you came from." Their gaze made me feel uncomfortable, an intruder in their world.

The men wore white tunics or were scantily dressed in loincloths, or the long wrapped around material tucked in at their waist. Some men had turbines on their heads and they all appeared to have mustaches. No one seemed to be smiling; only staring intently at me. I wanted to tell them, "I don't know what I am doing here either. This is not my choice."

I was seeing and feeling poverty and it was beyond what I had expected and envisioned. Nothing could have prepared me for the vast feeling of hopelessness and gloominess. I kept trying to reassure myself, "It's okay; everything will be okay."

Riding in our air-conditioned bus and driving through the dirt roads of Varanasi, the poverty was vast, compact, and intense. The streets were crowded with makeshift huts and tents. People were sleeping on the dirt road which led to the hotel. The streets were brimming with people living beyond poverty conditions. There was barely enough room for the bus to drive through. Begging barefoot children surrounded us as we got off the bus. The air was stifling with heat, mixed with that unfamiliar odor.

Soon I was walking the streets and could not believe what I was seeing. Beggars of all ages surrounded me. Cows were wandering the streets. Old men peddling rickshaws were everywhere. The men were very thin, of short stature and had bare feet. They wore the much seen white loincloth. They reminded me of Gandhi.

People would be poking their heads out of their makeshift huts, uncannily knowing there was an intruder walking by. Women were cooking on open campfires on the side of the dirt roads. Barefoot children surrounded it patiently waiting to eat the food.

The yelling vendors muffled the voices of the people who lived in the streets. The unbearable smell of poverty, feces, urine, and garbage was suffocating.

I was feeling like a failure before I began. "Lord," I whispered, "what can my measly $4,500 do in comparison to the devastation I am seeing. The money I brought is a mere grain of sand compared to this massive mountain of poverty and chaos." I inwardly begged, "God I do not want to fail you. I need help." I had a responsibility to God and I did not know where I could possibly begin. The child within was forever present.

As I walked the dirt roads, I became immersed in what I was seeing and I started to cry inside. It felt as though someone was walking with me and seeing what I was seeing and saying, *Look what has happened to my children.*

I had felt God's love and now I had a glimpse of His compassion. This was a knowing beyond any reasonable explanation. With gentleness and sadness, it seemed as though this turmoil had significance and purpose. The pain I was experiencing was different—raw and the intensity was deep. It would not let up; it was overwhelming and bombarding every fiber of my body. All my emotions were in turmoil and seemed to be screaming inside of me with a devastating and debilitating pain.

I felt completely alone with what I was experiencing. I could not stop the pain and the tears of frustration eventually flowed out. The magnitude of poverty, isolation, and the feeling of abandonment, hopelessness, and helplessness were agonizing and beyond what I could endure. Neither the professors nor the students knew how to help me. I would wander in and out of the students' rooms crying. They would look at me, put their hands up in sympathy, and not know what to say or do. My fellow travelers were having an adventure and were excited to be there. The reality of poverty did not seem to affect them the way it was overpowering me.

Professor Suzanne spent hours trying to help me cope with the pain, but the tears would not stop. "Your money will do much good," she said over and over trying to reassure me.

"How can the measly amount of money I brought do any good in the face of all this deprivation?" I would moan back.

I began to question and doubt my reasons for being in India. "Had I made a mistake? Could I have imagined my spiritual experiences? Could I have come half way around the world for nothing? Could God have made a mistake in choosing me? Where can I possibly begin?" These questions and thoughts of frustrations, mingled with tears, were intolerable.

"I can't take this, I'm going home," I informed my professors after days of crying.

I got up early the following morning and went for a walk down a dirt road, after a night of tears, doubts, and frustrations. I stumbled upon a Catholic church, the only one I would ever see in my travels in India. It was there, a comfort and familiar sight that I needed, just at the right moment. It was a beautiful vision to my eyes. As I walked in I saw on each side of the altar two large open windows and sheer curtains billowing in the breeze. It was sunny and peaceful. There was a large crucifix suspended in the middle of the altar.

I stared at it in shock and then marched down the aisle. Looking up at the crucifix, pointing my finger at it, I screamed, "We had a deal! No pain! You have two choices. Either you take this pain away or I am going home. I can't handle this anguish."

Painful wailing sounds came from the depth of my core as I crumbled to the floor and sobbed uncontrollably. Unbelievable sounds of pain were unleashed from within. There were feelings of letting out and letting go.

Suddenly, gentleness and love seemed to enfold me and the tears subsided. I became aware of the silence within me. There was a presence in the quietness, as overwhelming love and calmness filled me. I relinquished myself to these incredible feelings.

I stayed squatted on my knees with my forehead pressed on the cold stone floor for some time. I did not want to move for fear of losing this soothing feeling of serenity and peace. It was beyond the reality of understanding or explaining. There was a soothing feeling of being embraced and loved. I understood—God had chosen me to stay and I surrendered.

I walked out of the church. All the pain and confusion were removed. I was free from the burdens I had been carrying. The rays of sunlight bathed my body and soul. I stood there and allowed the feelings of incredible light to touch the very depth of me. Every fiber of my being was freed as I finally walked back to the hotel. There was a feeling of incredible bliss within me.

The group was at breakfast when I got back to the hotel. I joined in the laughter and teasing with my fellow travelers. I recall how the professors were looking at me intently, with a look of puzzlement, from the other end of the table at which we were sitting. At the time, I could not understand why they looked at me in that way. It was as though the pain that I had experienced in the last few days and the incidents of the last hour had never occurred and were erased from my mind.

It was only in retrospect, when I got back home to the United States, that I realized how the events had played out. I had to purge, not only the pain of the poverty I was experiencing, but also the accumulated layers of pain in my life. I had to de-emphasize the humanism in me so I could become more present in the essence of being in the now. This was so I could experience and understand, without previous attachments, perceptions, and expectations, to fulfill what I had been sent to accomplish. I was transformed to see and experience my present reality in Truth. I had to relinquish me in order to gain something more profound and real. The severing of my humanism was painful but necessary to continue with this unknown journey.

LIFE IN THE STREETS

The group and I settled in a hotel in the middle of what I soon realized was organized chaos. The hotel was located on a corner of three dirt roads. In the mornings, we had classes in one of the hotel rooms and afternoons we were off to explore and wander around. At this location, we studied the Hindi Language and history of the locations we were to visit the following day. The students did not seem to have any problem learning the language, especially Patrick. I struggled and learned only a few words. I never thought of the significance it could have, had I learned more; and yet, it was not necessary. I was connecting in the most basic and significant way, from the essence within my being.

One morning after breakfast, I sat on the steps of the hotel and noticed two young girls rushing to get to an area across the road. A hotel employee had just thrown garbage on top of a pile of more garbage. Their ages could have been four and six. I noticed they were rushing to get to the garbage before the cows did. The young girls had to step aside and allow the cows to take their fill; otherwise, they would have been trampled.

Cows are considered sacred by religions in India and allowed to roam freely. The concept is that all creatures have a soul. Killing any animal would be obstructing the natural cycle of birth and death. The unnatural death of that creature would have to be reborn in that same form to complete the cycle of reincarnation.

The stench was pungent with a suffocating smell of waste and decay. I was gagging, as I went over to meet the young girls. They were so tiny and their faces expressed such innocence. Their vivid eyes seemed to pierce my heart. They had short rumpled hair, shabby dirty dresses, and were barefoot of course. The older child held the hand of the younger child and both shyly stood there as I tried to converse with them. Since they did not speak English, I conversed with hand signals and smiles. Their innocent timid smiles yanked at my heart.

After that morning, I would wrap my breakfast and dinner, food that could be wrapped, and brought it to them. They knew when I would be coming out and they watched for me. As soon as they saw me, they would come running over. They never begged. They shyly put their hands out for the food and gave me a wonderful smile as my reward. For three weeks they did not go without food and I did not see them searching in the pile of garbage.

I knew they lived on the other side of the garbage pile, in a makeshift tent with their father and mother, on top of a stream. A small flat contraption was built over the stream for them to live on. Investigating one day, I realized that the stream was liquid waste. There were so many bugs and worms moving that it had appeared to be flowing water. I ached for those precious little girls.

One morning, I brought Bipina with me to translate. Bipina was born in India and brought to America when she was a child. I am sure this trip back to her birthplace had great significance for her.

She translated that the father had tuberculosis and could not afford the medicine. Aaron, another fellow traveler and I, purchased medicine from a drugstore. I was concerned that if we gave the father the money, he would not buy the medicine but save it for other necessities. I needed him healthy so he could take care of those little girls. Aaron and I gave the mother a cooking pot and floor mats as well.

The market places were packed with yelling vendors, the means of creating a living. Their struggles and the simplicity to endure were in the open dirt roads. Their creativity and inventiveness gave them the resources to survive against all odds and barriers.

The vendors and little shops were set up along the roads. There were garment sections, in the open with overstuffed racks, dividing a vendor from one another. There were live chickens, goats, and lambs ready to be slaughtered for the buyer. Sickly wild dogs would be wandering around begging for scraps but keeping their distance. Vendors were cooking food in the streets on open flames and selling to the multitudes of people in the crowded streets. Our group had been warned not to eat from the vendors, due to possible contamination, lack of sanitation and refrigeration.

Men would be sitting under trees, their faces lathered with soap for shaving or having their hair cut; young entrepreneurs had set up shop with only a chair, an ingenious way of making a living. A young dentist would be practicing his trade under a tree with a stool for his patient to sit on. The shoe repairperson had his little stool and spot, as he pounded away on my shoe, while I waited near by.

They were eager to take my money. They came rushing at me whenever I walked the streets. I started laughing one day, as I twirled around and counted the vendors surrounding me. There were twelve of them; all shoving and trying to out-talk the other. Understanding the reasons for my amusement and the absurdity of the circumstance, they too joined the laughter. They stopped yelling for a moment, as they smiled and posed, as I had our picture taken. As soon as the camera clicked, they instantly started yelling and shoving each other, trying to get my attention again.

There was an unspoken rule, I soon became aware of, which all vendors seemed to observe. As soon as someone got my attention and made a connection, the others would step aside. I always looked around and begged God to guide me to whoever needed the money most. That individual's face would light up and smile from ear to ear when I started conversing with him. He knew he got me! Everyone would politely stand within earshot, with their back half turned. I knew they were listening to everything that was going on and waiting for that transaction to finish.

I tried to linger with these exchanges and had a good time with them. It appeared that they were enjoying the interaction and attention as well. Then began the haggling, each of us going back and forth. I was used to haggling; after all, I am Italian. There was fun, laughter, and challenge as we conversed in different languages, trying to outwit each other. It was amazing how many of them spoke some English. They knew enough to be able to make the transaction. I always planned to spend some money every day and would only bring so much with me. I was afraid to bring more, because I would have spent more. I understood that if they made a few dollars that day, they were happy and had earned their pay without begging. I could see their eagerness in trying to succeed at life even with all the obstacles they had in their way.

As soon as I completed my transaction, the ones that had been standing by would come rushing at me yelling, minus the one who was walking away, smiling and counting his money. Who knows how many more came to join the group, in the hopes that they would be the next lucky person. They were not selling much, just trinkets.

I soon learned that in India there is no one to provide for the elderly. They count on the children they have born to provide for them in their old age. The more children they have, the better their life could be, when they are no longer able to go out and find a way to make a living. At the same time, the more children they have the harder it is to provide for them. It is such a sad paradox. There is no room for the old in the streets, there are too many young adults, and the elders are pushed aside. The old are just as heartbreaking to see as the children are.

Aaron and I were out in the market one day when I heard him exclaim, "Might has right," as everyone stepped aside for an elephant to go by. He was right. The weak had to step aside, in order for the young and the strong to survive.

I never knew what I would absorb in a day, as each one was different. My soul and eyes were open as I captured the essence of both the people and India.

THE POOREST OF THE POOR

It had taken me a while to accept a ride from the rickshaw, until Heather informed me that my hesitation was preventing the old men from making a living. I reluctantly gave in. The men who rode these bicycle contraptions were frail and old. I felt bad and guilty getting into the rickshaw. I recall one incident where I was being bicycled to the market place and the man peddling was struggling up a hill. I got out of the cart and started to push. He stopped, gave me his hand, and gently walked me back into the cart. A three-wheel motor vehicle drove by, slowed up, and the old man grabbed onto the vehicle, which pulled us up the hill. "The poor helping the poor," I thought. They help each other, whenever they can. They have pride, but when necessary, they will accept a helping hand.

One day I noticed that not many people went down a street that was located on the left side of the hotel. I roamed down there one day and understood the reason. A group of lepers lived there. Men, women, and children had nubs for fingers, or half of their faces eaten away. They covered up and moved away from me with their dark eyes darting. With curiosity, they followed but kept their distance. I could not turn away from their deprivation and desolate conditions. My heart was torn at what I was witnessing. I had to do something.

I went back to the hotel and bought rice and lentils, which the students and I packaged into small parcels. The students each took parcels to hand out to the people along the road. I did not ask them to go with me to feed the lepers, feeling that it was *my* responsibility. People often ask, "Weren't you afraid of them?" Fear never entered my mind. The desire to help was greater.

I hired a rickshaw and instructed him to go down the dirt road where the lepers were living. I saw a group of women and children milling around and I started handing out the dry goods to them. Immediately I was swarmed with a crowd of men and women. The men were aggressive while the women locked their eyes with mine, begging for me to give them the food. I tried to hand the food to the women. The men were shoving, yelling, and grabbing at me. It was impossible to see whose hand it was. I was frustrated. This became a devastating and humbling experience. I was overwhelmed with feelings of hopelessness and helplessness. It really did not matter; the men probably had families too.

This would be a lesson that would reinforce an opportunity that would later open ideas. I went back to the hotel with feelings of powerlessness from not being able to feed them all. How could I? Back at the hotel, I put the covers over my head and did not come out for the rest of the day. I felt empty.

Children were soon following me around. I had become a familiar figure and the pied piper of children. It seemed that one child would be waiting by the hotel steps and as soon as I came out, a group of children would suddenly appear. I have no idea how they knew that I had appeared. One little girl stood out in the group. She was so tiny and had the brightest eyes in her little round face. Her smile out-shone her raggedy appearance. She always wore the same dress and was barefoot, of course. She would be smiling, with her hip extended out on one side, carrying an over-grown toddler. She kept up with the others, never letting go of who I assumed was her sibling. Her parents probably worked in the hotel.

All the children had infectious smiles and happy dispositions. They had shiny black hair, with innocent bright eyes and golden brown little faces. The children were dressed in hand-me-down American clothes. The boys wore shorts and shirts and the little girls wore short dresses. Most likely, these were clothes that tourists from various parts of the world had handed out. I too had brought two suitcases full of children's clothes. I had been instructed by my professors not to hand them out until our group was ready to leave the area. Otherwise the children would swarm me when I came out of the hotel. It did not matter to the children; they still followed and ran around, yelling "Jozee, Jozee". I could not believe the love and connection we had made with each other, in only two short weeks.

Towards the end of our stay in Varanasi, I bought 50 pairs of flip-flops and handed them out to the children surrounding me. It was breathtaking to see them so excited over a pair of flip-flops. The next day I was bewildered, as they showed up barefoot again. Professor Ashok explained that they either sold them or kept them to use for special occasions. I was astounded by the importance of those flip-flops.

Coming out of the hotel one morning, I saw the mother of the two little girls, screaming and hitting a young girl of about fifteen. The young girl was holding a chubby baby boy in her arms. She was slender, with big almond eyes, and was dressed in a worn-out dirty blue sari. The baby was quiet in the young mother's arms, as the older mother shoved her. The young mother stood there with sadness on her face as the older woman continued to pound her. I started screaming at the older mother and grabbed her arm trying to stop her. Noticing my distress, she stopped and motioned the young mother to give her the baby. The young mother consented and handed him over. Cradling and rocking the baby in her arms, the older mother smiled at me. I understood, she was not going to hurt the baby. I grabbed each of their arms and motioned for them to stay there.

I ran back to the hotel and asked Bipina to come with me. Bipina translated, "Her husband, the father of the two little girls, fathered the baby of this young girl. The mother is not angry at the baby but at the young mother."

My reaction was anger; "Maybe I shouldn't have bought medicine for the father. Didn't he have anything better to do?" I wailed at Bipina.

I was bewildered with the father. I could not believe nor understand why he would put such a burden on two families. I walked away, not wanting to hear any more.

Walking around Varanasi, I pondered the reasons for my anger. "Was I displacing my anger because of my own marital morale? Was I judging on my own expectations and values? Because of my convictions would I rather have the father die?"

I questioned, "Who am I to say what is morally wrong or right?" I had never really pondered this cliché before.

There was a gradual acceptance that I did not have the right to pass moral judgment on another human spirit. What right did I have to say that the baby boy should not have life? How do I know the purpose that child has to fulfill? What right do I have to place my moral expectations on the father?

It soon became apparent that I had no right to judge or place my expectations on another human soul. This new non-judgmental knowledge, with no limitations or boundaries, felt as though another veil had been removed from my inner eyes. I was seeing and feeling with my authentic self.

There was direct transformation within me, an awakening. I became conscious of the awareness of this acceptance. It was as though I was watching the watcher being watched, as I was becoming more of the essence of me.

As time went on I stopped seeing the poverty and started seeing what was presented before me. I saw the simplicity and beauty that was actually there. I felt love and a connection to the people.

The people in the area became familiar at seeing me wandering around. They would sit up from where they were sleeping and wave or offer to share food from what they were cooking in an outdoor fire. They seemed to be teasing and trying to speak to me with hand signals and big toothless smiles. They were so kind. The love they extended was real, given freely, and shone brightly. Amazingly, it overshadowed the deprivation. I had felt their pain and now I was feeling their simple joy. I was experiencing the moment and the now. There was neither past nor future, just the present experience and moment.

A group of young women were bathing one morning, near a water spigot. They were teasing, splashing, and laughing with each other. It was a wonderful exchange of the moment, which I became a part of, as they tried to get me to join in their morning ritual. We connected in the simplest way; we have the same spirit—one human race—one human being. I was already part of them; and therefore, I was part of India and India was part of me. I was seeing and feeling India through their eyes and not mine. I was home.

Attached to the hotel was a low stone wall. Behind the wall was a small hut with a group of various generations living together. In the evenings I watched as they cooked and ate their meal while sitting or squatting around the campfire. The evening meal was the only meal I saw them eat together. One morning I watched a young girl from my window, who appeared to be the only one left behind after the others had gone to work. I was mesmerized as I watched the skill that she displayed. The young woman cleansed her body and changed her clothes without ever exposing herself. I came away with the realization that the people of India play out their lives in the open. There are no walls to hide behind.

Professor Ashok arranged for us to visit a middle class family. He explained to them who we were and what we were doing in India. They smiled broadly at us and exchanged pleasantries with the Professors. The women wore colorful saris in bright blue and red silk. Their feet were decorated with rings and colored toenails. Their hair was shiny and slicked back. Their bright eyes were outlined in black, enhancing their exotic features. The young children were dressed in American clothing and their eyes were over-emphasized in black, meant to ward off spirits. The young male members wore creamy colored white trousers and matching crisp shirts. The older male members wore the usual dhoti, material wrapped and draped over the shoulder.

It was a sparse room. In the corner were low stumps and bare wood for beds, no tables or chairs; they sit or squat on the dirt floors on top of mats. There was a stand-up open fire on the opposite corner used for cooking.

"This is middle class?" I thought. Now I understood what Mother Theresa meant when she said, "The Indian people are the poorest of the poor."

One day while roaming along a dirt road I noticed an old woman making cow patties. She mixed them with straw. They would be placed on the roof and the sides of the hut to keep out the sun and provide warmth at night. The cow patties were used for cooking and other purposes which I was later to learn. There was joy in that thin wrinkled face. She was at one with the simple task that she was performing. Her big warm smile was contagious as she worked on those patties, back and forth slapping from one hand to the other, as though she was making tortillas. There was no attachment to what she was doing or judgment to her act, just being in the moment of Being. This strange incredible scene was just another day for her. It revealed and opened volumes within me. I was experiencing the moments with my authentic-self.

At various times I contemplated the fact that I did not seem to be accomplishing much. I would wonder, "Is this why I am here Lord? Am I doing what you want me to do? How will I know what it is that I am supposed to do? How will I know that I have done what you sent me to do?" No answers ever came. I became immersed in the life of India and the people.

GANGA RIVER

The rivers in India are considered holy. On one of our excursions we left early in the morning for a boat ride on the most sacred river of all rivers in India, the Ganga. Hindus from various parts of India and the world, while alive or at death, must pilgrimage to the Ganga River. The belief is that they will break the cycle of reincarnation by having their ashes or body parts thrown in the river. They believe, also, that bathing in the Ganga River will remove their sins.

Our group was instructed not to put our hands in the water because it is one of the most polluted rivers in the world. There, at the edge of the river, was a large platform with wide cement steps that led to the top; this was for cremation. It looked like one of those tall sacrifice platforms that one sees in a black and white film. There was a smell of smoldering fire in the air and smoke was rising from the top of the platform. Some of my fellow travelers rushed to the top of the cremation tower. I did not have the courage to do that. I was afraid of what I might see.

We went into various small boats that floated the group down the river. We were given lighted votive candles to place on the river, in memory of our departed loved ones. I meditated on my Nonno and Nonna, whispering to them that I loved and missed them. There were thousands of bright votive candles floating on the river, which twinkled and added to the mystery and pageantry.

I looked at the riverbank. It was alive and swarming with thousands of people, all in colorful clothing. There were bathers and ascetic priests called sadhus, performing religious rites. Some sadhus appeared to have ashes on their naked bodies and faces. Others were naked, covered with tattoos. There were women fully clothed, bathing or washing clothes on the shores, and banging the clothing on stones. The view boggled my mind; it was mesmerizing.

We returned from where we started, near the cremation platform. I seemed to have found the courage to walk up those long stairs. As I started climbing them, I passed elderly people sitting or squatting at the corners of the steps. Later I learned that they were waiting to die and had traveled to be there, in order to have the privilege of being cremated at this holy site.

I reached the top and looked out. I could see below me the Ganga River on one side and the community on the opposite side of the platform. Somehow, I had expected that there would be a pit on top. Instead there was a wide, flat, cement slab. A group of men was sweeping it.

Hundreds of people are cremated on this sacred spot every day. The ashes and unburned body parts are disposed of in the river. People who cannot be cremated are pregnant woman, holy men, children, and people with certain diseases. Their bodies are weighted down with stones and dropped in the river. If someone dies before ever making the pilgrimage to the river, male family members will come, from various parts of India or the world, to dump the ashes or body parts into the Ganga River.

I looked out over the community; there were thousands of straw huts, small shops, vendors, and a milling of people below. I could hear chants, bells, vendors yelling, and the chatter of people. It was as though each unique sound blended into a harmonious symphony.

I started walking down those long steps. I felt a strong steady pressure on top of my head. It was not painful but was uncomfortable. I felt as though I was floating down the steps. I felt disorientated. The chaos of the scene and the many sounds coming from it created a state of confusion in my head. Suddenly it all stopped. This is one of the busiest and noisiest places in India; yet, I did not hear a sound. Everything became quiet and my breathing was all I heard. The pressure continued on my head. I reached the bottom of the stairs and started walking among the people. They looked at me and parted like the red sea, as I walked down the path that opened before me. I noticed that the people in front held the other people back, with their arms stretched out where I was walking. I have no idea what they saw when they looked at me, which kept them away. I did not understand what was happening or why I was feeling so strange and disoriented.

Suddenly I heard a small noise in the distance; it got louder and louder, and then rushed in. Wherever I walked that day, people would look at me and put their head down. They kept their distance. Their usual procedure of rushing at me did not happen. For the rest of the day I continued to feel disoriented.

I have since understood the potential reasoning for this experience. Since there are many people cremated in this location, the spirit, the energy, the soul is strong. It is sacred ground. I was open and I felt the energy forces from the souls that had been cremated in that location. Their energy had affected my energy. Perhaps the people in this area were aware of this affect and understood what was happening. They knew not to interfere.

On one of our other excursions, we stopped at a gas station. The shop owner had a nice little shop with food, trinkets, and a restroom. The establishment was small, neat, and clean. "There seems to be some progress in the country, but certainly not enough that it makes a dent compared to the magnitude of the poverty," I said to Professor Suzanne.

Professor Ashok complemented the shopkeeper on his establishment. The shopkeeper beamed, he was very proud. I could see that Professor Ashok's words meant so much to him. "A helping hand and kind words could go such a long way," I said to Professor Ashok.

We went to a factory on a side street. Someone took us there, otherwise, we would not have known of its existence. Boys, as young as seven, were in dark basement sewing, with only a small narrow window by the ceiling for light. They turned on the light so our group could see. I did not understand the conversation that Professor Ashok had with the shop owner, since their exchange was in their native language. It was apparent by the tone of his voice that Professor Ashok was upset. My fellow travelers and I were subdued with what was obvious, the abuse of children. We watched in silence and walked out with our heads down. There was a feeling of guilt, shame, and anger.

Professor Ashok later explained to the group that child labor, as young as five years old, is a big problem in India. Their childhood and education are robbed. They work ten to twelve hours a day for as little as fifty cents. These children are treated as slaves. They work to support their families and to learn a trade. There are over 3 million children living in the streets and 150 million working as bonded laborers, some in hazardous conditions.

"In a perverse way, these children feel lucky to have a job," I thought.

John asked, "Why do the parents allow this?"

"Parents do not understand, this is all they know," one of the professors stated.

"When does the cycle break?" I asked.

Professor Ashok shrugged his shoulders, "I don't know."

We had studied, experienced, and interacted with the people in Varanasi for three weeks; it was the end of September, time for our group to leave. Our tour bus came and was waiting outside the hotel to pick us up. Many children, people from the community, and staff from the hotel were standing outside to say good-by.

As I was getting ready to climb in the bus to leave for New Delhi, I saw the two little girls that I had befriended. The mother was holding the baby of the young girl that her husband had fathered. At various times during our stay, I had seen her with the baby. Somehow, they must have come to some arrangement or acceptance of their circumstances.

Bipina came up to me and said, "The mother of the two little girls came to speak to you. She has a question to ask you."

Bipina translated what the woman was saying, "Who is going to feed my children now that you are leaving?"

I had no answers for her. I could only shake my head in shame and sadness. I quickly got on the bus.

I looked at those two beautiful little girls, shyly waving at me, as our bus pulled away. I have often wondered what happened to them. Their angelic faces and beautiful shy smiles are engraved on my heart.

I had experienced and learned so much in three weeks. As we drove away, I thought that I was ready to face and acknowledge the rest of the trip.

Nothing could have prepared me for what was yet to come.

LEARN AND SERVE

We went to New Delhi next, as part of the *Learn and Serve Program*. The students had each chosen a place where they were going to volunteer for part of the three weeks we were to be in New Delhi. The one site not yet chosen was at a Spastic Society. Amber, another fellow traveler, and I arranged to go there together. Neither of us had any idea what to expect. It was a makeshift day school for children who were disabled. The day school was actually a house with small rooms. Children were dropped off every morning and picked up at night. Children would lie down or sit on floor mats or be in wheelchairs. The women who ran the center were very kind and took great care with the children. Amber and I spent our days interacting and feeding the children.

I will never forget two young girls, sisters, who were at the facility. They were 14 and 16 years old. The mother and father of these two young girls were college professors and only had the two daughters. I met the mother every morning as she dropped off her daughters. The mother spoke some English and was able to converse with me. She informed me that she and her husband were actively involved in raising money to build a permanent school and dormitory for these children. She said, "I know that there is going to come a time when I won't be able to take care of my daughters. What is going to happen to them if my husband and I die before they do? The relatives do not want them, they are a burden, and would be exposed to abuse. Children with cerebral palsy need their own home where they will be safe."

One morning I came to the school to discover that one of the girls was sick. I could see the pain in her eyes, as she lay on the floor mat. Wordlessly, she pleaded with sadness in her eyes for her mother to stay as she watched her mother walk away to go to work. There was a person trapped in her body who could not cooperate with her mind. Hers eyes spoke for her and they spoke of pain and fear. I had to walk away.

I had time to ponder about the parents and why they had been dealt this hand in life. Why did God give this family this pain, beyond human endurance? Unusual thoughts came to me. *Could this be their chosen journey? The parents and the children are on this journey together in order to help build the cerebral palsy home. Their journey is for the gain of others. They are God's angels on earth to do His work. In spirit, they know this, but in human spirit, they do not. This is their walk.*

Even though these thoughts were unusual, somehow they were not strange to me. I knew that they added to the collective knowledge of my human spirit. These thoughts felt as though they had always been there and now was the time to remember them. I donated $500 towards the building of the school and home for the disabled. This would open ideas for me to help them later.

While in New Delhi, I befriended a businessman, Prahn Mehata, a Kodak distributor. He donated $500 to the Children's India Fund, after hearing of my raising money for the children.

Prahn took me to visit his farm one day. He was very proud of his vegetable garden. Prahn explained that he was actively involved in the building of an elementary school for girls.

I asked him, "Why just for girls and not boys as well?"

He went on to explain, "Male sons work and bring money into the household and provide for their elderly parents. Young females cannot go out to work; and therefore, do not bring anything to the household. Their purpose in life is to get married and produce sons. The requirement of parents is to deliver an unblemished daughter. Most schools are a distance away and filled with male teachers and students. The mere fact that the female would be exposed to males, cannot guarantee that she is pure. If the daughter did not marry, she would become a burden and humiliation to her family. Because of this thinking and way of life, parents are not likely to send their daughters to school."

"What about when they are married? Do these women have a voice?" I asked.

"No—because they do not have the resources to support themselves, so they become subjective to their husband, his family, and the possibility of being mistreated," Prahn explained.

"Why do women allow this to happen?" I asked.

"It is engrained into their belief and way of life," Prahn said. "Even the women, accept their path in life. This is all they know and understand."

"Can anything be done?" I asked.

"Yes! There is a movement, among the educated men and women of India, to educate young girls. We believe that if a woman becomes educated, it will ensure that all her children become educated. The belief being, if you educate a woman, you educate a family."

"So education is the pathway for women and children to become liberated and women must be educated first in order to insure that her children are educated. Education will provide for positive change and liberation for the women and children of India," I said to Prahn.

"Yes and educated women understand this," He said.

"Certainly, a country that prides itself in being the first nation to provide equality to women has fallen short of that reality," I said in wonderment.

"This is a country of many contradictions," Prahn said.

I was thrilled to donate the $500 back to Prahn for the school for girls, in New Delhi, which was in the process of opening.

It was later that I realized I had reached the goal of $5,000, the amount that Rosa and I had vowed to raise for the children of India.

While we were in New Delhi, the two college professors went ahead to Dundlod, located in Rajasthan, to prepare for our next phase of the trip. The location where we were to stay was a fort or castle turned into a hotel by the royal family. The professors informed Prince Bonnie, that a student had brought money.

"How can we utilize this money to benefit the community?" asked Professor Ashok.

Sunina, the manager of the establishment said, "There are many children from the Untouchable caste that do not go to school. Can a school be started for them?"

When the professors returned, they informed me of the idea to start a school for the Untouchable children. I readily agreed.

I asked Professor Ashok, "What are the Untouchable children?"

Professor Ashok went on to explain, "The caste system is levels of status in the Indian culture. The people are born into a level of a caste and the individual marries and dies within their caste. The caste determines their place in society. There are four major castes: Brahmins—priests, Kshatriyas—warriors and rulers, Vaishyas—merchants, and Shudras-workers. The three higher castes are accepted in society and have more opportunities in life. The Shudras are better known as the Untouchables, and of the lowest class. They do the manual labor, are considered impure, and are therefore, outcasts of society. Even though the government, in the 1950's, abolished the caste system, time has stood still in small communities. In the past, if the shadow of an Untouchable person touched someone from the higher caste, the higher caste person would have to cleanse himself to remove the infringement on his body. Of course, they also believe that if the Untouchables don't do the manual work, who will?"

"Why don't the Untouchable people move from where they live and not tell what caste they belonged to?" I asked.

"It's not that easy. The people of India are not mobile like they are in the United States. Besides the caste system is engrained into their belief and way of life. It is an integral part of their culture, life, and Hindu philosophy, of Dharma, Karma, and Reincarnation. The caste system divides and defines them, as to who they are in life and who they will be in death. The people who belong to the Untouchable caste are also not considered capable of learning."

"Do the people in Dundlod want the school to succeed and the children to learn?" I asked.

"We may run into some problems. It is hard to say."

"I am so glad we are going to do something for the children."

Professor Suzanne tried to anticipate the needs of the children and the school. While we were in New Delhi, we bought books, school supplies, and mats for the children to sit on, from the Children's India Fund money.

INDO-INTERNATIONAL SCHOOL

At the end of October, we arrived at Dundlod, located in Jhunjhunu, district of Rajasthan in the northern part of India. Never could I have imagined the impact the community of Dundlod, which is located in the middle of the desert, would have on my life and I on theirs.

As our bus was taking us down a dirt road, at what appeared to be the main road in Dundlod, I could see a medieval castle at the end of the road. Like most communities in India, Dundlod was poor. Our bus drove past two large doors and into an open courtyard. A majestic castle stood in front of us. Our group was eager to get off the bus after a long dusty, bumpy ride, and we quickly scrambled out.

I stood in the courtyard and surveyed my surroundings. A stonewall surrounded the castle and horse stables were attached to the courtyard walls. The stables appeared to be empty. These stables would play a significant transformation to this community. Large stone statues that were scattered in the courtyard gave the surroundings an eerie feeling from the past. An old cannon stood on the side of the courtyard, which represented the history gone by. I wondered if it had been used hundreds of years ago against the British people, who colonized India. Impressive large stone chairs were strategically placed in the courtyard. I walked up the steps, onto a wide outside entryway, and walked past billowing long curtains and into the castle. Directly inside stood two imposing royal thrones with high backs and intricate armrests inlaid with gold. I sat on the throne and placed my arms on the armrests. I settled in the plush gold embroidered cushions and imagined the history that must have been.

I was informed that Kesari Singh built the castle in 1750 A.D. He was the ancestor of our host, Kanwar Raghuvendra Singh, better known as Prince Bonnie. There were family portraits of Prince Bonnie's ancestors in various rooms, which were filled with antique furniture, reminiscent of the royal era.

Our group was staying in what had been the living quarters for the women. There was a small separate courtyard in the center of that compound. The castle was a fascinating place for our group. We were soon exploring and found many narrow stairways that connected to various parts of the castle. I discovered a room with a multitude of sheer curtains overlooking the royal throne room. I was informed it was the room where women had observed in obscurity, as the king and queen below dealt with people from the community or entertained visiting guests. My fellow travelers and I found our own tower to congregate in, high in the castle overlooking the town on one side and the desert on the other.

Prince Bonnie was a tall man with piercing blue eyes and jet-black hair. He had a quick smile under his thick mustache and a hearty laugh. He reminded me of the actor, Omar Sharif, only royal. I loved looking at his shoes. They looked like Aladdin's, with curled toes. He laughed when he told me that tourists took pictures of them.

Prince Bonnie had turned part of the castle into a hotel in order to provide a living for his family, wife and two daughters. He also conducted group horse safaris in the desert at various times of the year. Prince Bonnie explained that his horse farm was not far from the castle and offered to show it to us.

Prince Bonnie took the professors and me in his jeep to see the stables. The stables were filled with a special breed of horses that I had never seen. Walking through the tackle room there were various poster-size pictures of Prince Bonnie on horseback. The tackle room opened onto the courtyard where the horses were kept. The horses had their own stall which was connected on two sides to the corral. As I walked down the middle of the corral, the horses poked their heads out over the gates and watched us. They were majestic.

"I have never seen this breed of horses before. What are they?" I asked Prince Bonnie.

"These horses are called Marwari; they are a cross of our Indian ponies and Arabian horses. They are indigenous to India. This breed has almost become extinct. I am working towards preserving them," Prince Bonnie said.

"Their ears are so distinct," I said. "They curve up and inward and some of the tips touch."

"That's one of the most distinguishing features of the Marwari horses. In the sixteenth century, my ancestors used them in battle. The Marwari showed great temperament and faced death bravely. My ancestors trained them to protect their masters from the enemy. These horses are a descendent of the war horses".

"That's an amazing story. They have such long eyelashes," I said.

"Yes, that is to protect them when they are out in the desert," Prince Bonnie explained. "People come from all over the world to join me and my team in the desert safaris so they can ride these magnificent horses."

"Wish I could take one back with me," I wistfully said.

"They are not exported out of the country, perhaps someday."

Princess Ganga, the Prince's wife, was a slender statuesque woman with shiny dark shoulder length hair and olive skin. I sensed the beauty and compassion in her big oval eyes. Her voice had a sing-song quality, which was pleasant to listen to. She was not from royal decent but she might as well have been. Princess Ganga did not spend much time at the castle, but she came that week because Prince Bonnie had informed her of our project. Princess Ganga lived with their two daughters in Jaipur, or better known as the Pink City of India. Princess Ganga had studied in America, returned to Jaipur, and opened a hearing clinic.

Amazingly, Professor Ashok had made many trips to Dundlod in the past with college groups; and yet, he was meeting Princess Ganga for the first time. The stage had been set and the new players were in place.

The professors and I discussed our plans, a free school for the Untouchable children, with Princess Ganga and Prince Bonnie. Princess Ganga turned to Prince Bonnie and said, "The royal family has never done anything for the people of Dundlod in five hundred years. This is a great opportunity for us to do something for them."

Besides the castle, the Prince's parents also had a home nearby. Professors Suzanne, Ashok, and I rode camels to their home. The home was a modest size. We entered a large room with long billowing veils in the entryway. King Rex was a portly man. He was jovial, exuberant, and full of stories of the royal family. He seemed to be enjoying our company.

Queen Jean was petite and quiet. She had fairer skin than most people that I had seen in India. Her sari was a light peach color, and on her shoulders was the usual veil that I had seen worn by women of India when they covered their faces. She had the same distinctive eyes that Prince Bonnie and King Rex had, a dark circle surrounding their blue eyes.

Queen Jean went about quietly instructing servants in the serving of tea and biscuits as we sat on enormous cushions in a circle. She sat quietly while her husband told stories of the castle and of his two brothers who also owned part of the castle.

"This is amazing," I thought. "I am sitting here with royalty." It was so interesting to hear the history of the royal family, the castle, and the community.

Soon I was roaming the village and again the children seemed to have found me. It was an incredible feeling to hear them chant,

"Jozee, Jozee" and smile. They had connected with me and I with them.

An old woman from the village donated the use of a cinder block room that was located on the outskirts of the community, out on the desert. Because the Prince had requested the use of the room, she readily agreed. It was rather amazing that the structure was not utilized and even more amazing that she gave us permission to use it for the Untouchable children.

The major team players, the professors, Princess Ganga, Prince Bonnie, and I, decided to call the school *Indo-International School.*

While a group of students, along with Professor Suzanne, was preparing the school, the rest of us started another project. A building foundation, which had never been finished, would serve for a community center and a place where travelers could spend the night.

Professor Ashok hired local bricklayers and purchased bricks from the Children's India Fund. Human hands passed the bricks from one member of our group to another. The students and I took turns working with the bricklayers as we watched the building going up. Camels, their mode of transportation, brought the bricks in carts from the quarry. It was amazing to see how the roof was made of straw. A skilled man worked on it daily. The students and I carried the roof to the foundation. Time, it seems, has stood still in this community, as it has in most of India. This was another world.

A little girl by the name of Indo seemed to have connected with me. She stole my heart as many of them did. She was five years old. She had short dark straight hair, with a chubby round face. Her eyes were as big as saucers fringed with long dark lashes. She smiled all the time and seemed so happy. Whenever Indo found an opportunity, she would come and sit on my lap and snuggle up. She was from the Untouchable caste. She was dressed in shabby American dresses and barefoot of course.

Princess Ganga explained, "The tourists who stay at the castle bring clothes for the children. I make sure the clothes are distributed to them. We have also instructed the children not to beg."

Meanwhile Professor Suzanne was interviewing prospective teachers. She hired a man, George, who would become instrumental with the school. George was from the southern part of India and was a pharmacist. He spoke English fluently. George was of medium build and height with dark olive skin, dark hair, and a mustache of course. He and his wife had a two-year-old daughter.

We held the first parents meeting in the schoolroom. We were sitting in a circle, on the floor of course, and Professor Ashok was discussing with mothers the importance of sending their children to school. A large shadow appeared at the opened door. It was Prince Bonnie. The women quickly covered their faces with veils and rushed out past him with their heads down. I was perplexed and stunned.

"What happened?" I asked Prince Bonnie.

He gave a hearty laugh and with a twinkle in his eye said, "They all rushed home to fix dinner for their husbands." I was later informed that they could not sit or look at the face of the royal family; they were from the Untouchable caste.

One day George informed me that his wife, Maura, who is a midwife, was going to deliver a baby soon. "I would like to be there when the baby arrives," I said. Sure enough, George came to get me that evening.

We rushed to the only medical facility, a clinic in the area. I saw a group of people standing outside a door, in a poorly lit hallway. They were smiling and excited at the anticipation of the new arrival to their family. George knocked at the door and it was opened. George said that he would return to walk me back to the castle. He left and Maura locked the door behind me after I stepped into a poorly lit room. Maura was a stout young woman in her mid thirties. She did not speak English. There was also an older woman in the room assisting her.

The room had one exposed light bulb hanging on an electric cord in the middle of the ceiling. In one corner was a cot with a young girl, in her late teens, who was about to deliver. It was a sparse room with a dirty sink on the opposite wall and a small raised wooden table in the middle.

The young girl endured the pain of childbirth in silence with only her head thrusting about. Maura and the young girl did not exchange words. I watched in silence as the baby's head crowned and then the body whooshed out. The baby gave a vigorous cry. It was a boy. I had never seen life come into the world from this perspective. It was an emotional moment for me. The assistant cleansed the baby by placing him underneath the faucet; the water was cold, the baby was screaming. There was no hot water. She wrapped him up in gauze fabric and placed him in my arms. I could not help but think that this child's first experience of life was shock and pain. It was such a beautiful, sad, and humbling experience. Tears were streaming down my face as he screamed in my arms. I had witnessed life come into the humbleness of his world. I walked over to the mother and showed her the baby. She gave a faint smile. Maura was still cleansing her.

I stumbled back to the castle in the dark. I was so emotionally moved from the experience that I forgot to wait for George. The next day George informed me that he had been concerned for my safety and had walked to the castle to insure that I had gotten back. After apologizing, I asked George if he could take me to see the baby. He took me to the young mother's home.

We entered a very sparse room with only a cot in the corner. The young mother was sitting on the cot with the baby in her arms. She wore a light pink sari. She was smiling at the baby in her arms. She seemed relaxed. The pains of childbirth were gone from her eyes and now they were filled with love. The young father, also in his late teens, was standing by very proudly and smiling. He was tall, of slender build, and had a mustache of course. He wore a dhoti. This was the young couple's first baby.

The young mother motioned to me to hold the baby. I gently took the baby from her arms and cradled him in mine. He was so precious. He had dark hair and a tiny pink face. He had on a plaid shirt and was bare bottomed. He was very alert and quiet. The fact did not escape me that I had been the first person to hold him. I whispered a prayer to God that He would take care of him.

The baby looked up at me as I rocked him in my arms and at that moment, George said, "His name is Shirag, which means a light that shines in the dark." I felt a connection to this child. I left the young couple some money.

When the time came to register children for the Indo-International School, many showed up. We could only accept forty-five for this very small barren room and they could only be members of the Untouchable caste. We had to turn many away. Their ages ranged from five years old to fourteen and they would all be working on the same subject at the same level. This would be a free school for the Untouchable children, which was unheard of in India.

I was choked up at seeing what the Children's India Fund had accomplished. The fund provided for two teachers' salary for three years and money for school supplies, as well as the money I had spent along the way. The money had gone far. The money was a mere grain of sand in the mountain of chaos and poverty, but that grain of sand had become a beacon of light on that mountain.

After being in Dundlod for two weeks, I was out of money from the fund. We were leaving Dundlod the next day. As I was falling asleep, questions and thoughts were bombarding my mind: I am out of money Lord. Did I accomplish what you wanted me to do? I want to go home, I miss my children. What am I doing here?

Amazingly, all the time I had been in India, over two months by now, I rarely thought about home. It seemed as though that part of my life had been erased. Contacting my children by phone was difficult. I had to find a location, which were called STD phone stations. I would go into a phone booth while they connected me from an adjacent room. The eleven hours time difference also presented a problem. Finding these locations and correlating to the time in the U.S. was difficult. Then I was lucky if we got connected. The problematic issues discouraged me from attempting to call home. It seemed as though I had to leave the past behind for so many reasons. I had to become immersed in the moment and the experiences of the reality of those moments. The fact that I was in India and not home with my children, where I felt I should have been, hit me hard that night. Suddenly I missed them so much and felt the pangs of separation from them. With no answers in sight, I finally fell asleep.

Early morning, I found myself, again, in the most astonishing dream reality. I was bending down, bottle-feeding a baby lamb. Next to the lamb, were feet in sandals, peering out of a white robe. Instinctively I knew it was Jesus. Next to Jesus was another individual with bare feet poking out of a white tunic. There was a wooden staff next to these bare feet. His identity was not revealed. Looking sideways, I understood my cousin Rosa was standing next to me holding a chubby baby girl in her arms, with its legs dangling. We were all facing Jesus and the man in the white tunic. I could not see any faces, only the lamb I was feeding before me.

The following spring Rosa gave birth to a baby girl. She had gotten pregnant when I was in India and I was not aware of this knowledge. When I returned from India, I could not tell her the full vision I had of her and the baby, until the baby was born. Something would prevent me from voicing it or I would forget until I left her. Of all the names, she could have chosen she named her daughter Angela, which means angel in Italian. I feel that God rewarded Rosa for all the hard work she put into the Children's

India Fund. He gave her the greatest gift of all, a little girl, which she desperately wanted after having had two boys.

I opened my eyes and knew that I had gotten my answer—I had accomplished what God had sent me to do. *"Feed my lambs"*, God had said to me six months earlier in the church and here I was feeding the lamb, a symbol in the Christian religion meaning God's children. I understood that the school was the nourishment that was needed to feed the children. "I did accomplish what you wanted me to do, right Lord?" I still questioned. More affirmation was to come.

I had an urgent need to go out into the desert to be alone. I quietly got dressed in the dark, not wanting to wake up Amber, my fellow traveler. I could not find my sandals in the dark. I draped a shawl on my head and silently slipped out of the room. I walked quietly down the narrow stairway and into the empty predawn courtyard.

I was heading towards the castle door when I noticed that it was closed. All the time our group had been there, it had been wide open. How I am going to get out, I wondered. As I neared the castle door, I could make out a smaller door in the middle of the larger door. I put my left hand on the door and pushed. As I did, the vision I had four years earlier instantaneously flashed before me. This was the dream reality I had when the two angels appeared before me, saying they had been waiting for me. They had escorted me to a castle door which I opened with my left hand. The man inside gave me a gift and now I understood what that gift was. I realized I had just fulfilled what had to be done. This was an affirmation that I had accomplished the journey, which was to bring the gift of light to this remote village.

"This is where I am meant to be. I did accomplish what you wanted God," I whispered looking up into the heavens. Explicitly and without doubt, I knew these truths: There is no place on earth, at this moment in time that I am to be, other then here. The guilt of not being home, of not being where I thought I should have been, was lifted.

Walking out of the castle, I saw what looked like a worn-out path, leading away from the village and into the desert. I was lost in thoughts, amazed at the revelation and inner knowledge that was being revealed to me. There was a small group of trees in the distance and I veered off the path to sit underneath them. The sky had turned from light blue to a bright pink in the horizon. I noticed two young girls in the path I had walked, following a group of lambs. They are bringing them to grazing ground, I thought, as I hobbled around, trying to spread my shawl. I noticed they were giggling, covering their mouths, whispering to each other, and pointing at me. It did not take long to understand their humor and I too chuckled at myself. This would be my Bodhi tree, my tree of enlightenment. Leave it to me to pick a tree that sheds three-inch thorns.

Professor Ashok had informed us of the story of Prince Gautama Buddha, who relinquished his kingdom to seek the secrets of life, and to understand the reasons for suffering in the world. After years of searching for answers, he refused to go any further, and sat beneath a Bodhi tree. Looking within, in meditation, he allowed the spirit to flow for answers. When he came out of his meditation, he understood that suffering is universal and caused by either ignorance or greed. His belief was that to stop the suffering, we must stop what causes the suffering to others and to us. In order to follow his path, one must change the view of how one is living, to do only good things in the world, which I believe is the basis of all religions.

Sitting there, beneath my Bodhi Tree, I searched for understanding of my journey. I recalled the words that Joan said to me in Albany, which foretold that I would be going to another world. This was another affirmation of the prophecy of where I am, is where I am meant to be.

Suddenly Katherine came to my inner vision, and there too

was acknowledgement and understanding that she had prepared my soul for the path that I had just completed. Katherine had begun the awakening of my search that I instinctively knew was from within. My inner journey would take me to an outer journey. On my human level, I would not have been able to understand or been willing to accept the pain and transformation that was before me. On a spiritual level at that time, I knew these things, and I had agreed to fulfill the prophecy. Another veil was now removed from my inner eyes, revealing understanding and acceptance of my extraordinary journey.

I understood that the same two angels had been appearing from the time of my holy communion, when I was seven years old, and perhaps even before. They had been guiding me, and at various times in my life, they were people in my path to give me words of comfort, guidance, and enlightenment. There had been signposts throughout my life but I had not known how to read them. At my soul level, I understood. This had left a residue of acknowledgement and now in human terms I read the signs.

I saw how my life had been a series of events that would clear the path for me to be where I was that day. There had been stepping-stones placed in my path for me to follow. Sitting under my tree of enlightenment that morning, everything became clear.

I was humbled with all the revelations and still wondered, "Why me Lord? I am nobody. Couldn't someone else have been more accepting to understand what is now being revealed to me?" The child within was forever present, to put things into human perspective.

I watched the sunrise and it warmed my face. I felt the presence of God within. I noticed a figure in the distance striding towards me; my heart lurched. I knew it was a man, even though he had a blanket over his head covering his body. I heard words within saying, *"Be not be afraid."* Any trepidation vanished. As he approached, I placed my hand above my eyes, to shade them from the rising sun. It was sweet, gentle Luke, one of my fellow travelers. He also was out for a walk in the early morning.

"You look so radiant and luminous, like an angel sitting underneath that tree," he said. Those words leapt inside me as an acknowledgement. I felt a glow vibrating and resonating in my soul. These were strange words to hear and I understood, for one brief second in time, I had been God's angel on earth and had just completed His work.

Sitting all alone in the desert, away from my familiar surroundings, I felt more at home and at peace than I had ever felt in my life. There was a feeling of being complete and whole within my being. I thought of the vision I had that morning. I had inner knowledge that the man in sandals was Jesus but the identity of the barefoot man, holding the wooden staff, was not revealed. I did not have the urgency to know the answer. Perhaps I was not meant to know the answer at this time. It would be years before this knowledge would become known.

We prepared to leave Dundlod and, as usual, many of the people in the community including children came to say good-bye. I had connected with many people in Dundlod that have since become part of my life, such as Prince Bonnie, Princess Ganga, King Rex, Queen Jean, George, Indo, Shirag, and all the precious children.

Everything seemed to have culminated for me in Dundlod. As our bus was pulling away, I looked at the faces of the children surrounding the bus and I whispered, "I am done, I have completed what I was sent to do." How wrong could I be?

THE JAINS MONASTERY

Perhaps one of the most unusual places we visited was the Jains Monastery. We were to spend a week at this retreat. Professor Ashok had instructed the group about the history and teachings of Jain followers.

Professor Ashok explained that the beginnings of Jainism are traced to Var-dhamana Mahavira, who was born to a ruling family. When he was thirty, he abandoned his family and wealthy lifestyle. His belief was that by fasting he would purify his consciousness to learn the meaning of reality. When he achieved illumination, he spent the rest of his life meditating and coaching a group of disciples, who formed an organization following his beliefs. When Mahavira's work was completed, he starved himself to death. His deliberate death was highly esteemed.

The Professor went on to explain the belief system of the Jains. It is based on karma, in which all actions have a consequence that follows the soul from past lives into the present life. Past actions accumulate in the body. In order to break the cycle and not reincarnate over and over, they must not accumulate bad karma. Their belief is that the worst actions are violence against living things such as humans, animals, and plants. Their belief is that all living things are considered to have a soul. Some Jains wear masks to avoid accidentally ingesting small organisms. Some even walk with little brooms to sweep in front of them to clear any small insects that might be in their path. When the cycle of reincarnation is broken, they will achieve nirvana and become God.

Even with all the preparation that Professor Ashok had given us, I was still not prepared for what I was about to witness. Driving through the gates of the Jains monastery, in our air-conditioned bus, we saw a milling of people who looked like surgeons. The members wore long white tunics, masks covering their nose and mouth, sweeping little brooms in front of them. There were men, women, as well as children, all members of the monastery. There were hundreds of them walking around the manicured grounds.

Since they could not kill anything, I watched them go out in the morning with their little metal pails, begging for food in the small community outside the monastery gates. The Jains are vegetarians. It seems that they could eat what someone else prepared as long as they had not done the killing of the vegetables. At first, this seemed to me to be contradictory to their beliefs, even though I was not judging their actions. I realized that they justified it by not being responsible for the killing; and of course, they would starve if they did not eat. The simplicity of this action seems strange but the message is clear, *do not kill. There is sacredness in all life.*

I had learned many valuable lessons during my travels and here one was put to the test. Early mornings I would wake up and attend morning prayers in the open courtyard. There was a large stage where the head of the monastery sat. There were hundreds of people sitting on the ground chanting and looking upwards towards the stage. It was a remarkable sight. At times, I laughed at myself as I looked around me. There was a sea of people dressed in white, only their eyes showing above the masks. Then there was me, a blonde-haired, light-skinned woman sitting amongst them. I must have looked out of place. They were kind and accepting of me and made room on the ground for me to sit among them. I did not understand what was going on but felt a union with them and had a feeling that I belonged. I was experiencing Truth-that spirituality and the connection to a higher source are the same. I was walking the talk and this realization was another awakening to the reality of Being.

In the mornings, there would be young boys in the courtyard, heating up water in containers over gas burners. The hot water was used for mixing with cold water in our rooms, for personal cleansing in the bathrooms. There was a hole in our bathroom floor for the water to drain out, as I poured water over my head. The same hole was used as the toilet. By now we had gotten used to this during our travels in India. Toilet paper was scarce in most of India and we had brought our own. Aaron used to tease everyone that he was the most popular person in our group; he had brought an entire suitcase full of toilet paper.

Frequently, I would wake up at odd hours of the night and go walking in the monastery. It was so soothing and tranquil at those hours. I looked forward to going to bed so I could wake up for my walks. I would find the head of the monastery awake also at all hours of the night, having an audience with various people. There was a large room near the outdoor stage. Sheer curtains were part of the walls, which surrounded this room. They would blow in the breeze, which gave the room a gentleness, softness, and peacefulness. The head of the monastery was a heavyset man. He of course was dressed in a white tunic, sitting cross-legged on large cushions, on a small platform. His eyes, the only thing I could see of his face, had compassion in them while he listened patiently, quietly, and attentively. Men in the room, who seemed to be in charge, would be taking down notes and walking about, speaking in hushed tones to others who were waiting their turn.

When he would see me walking about and peeking through the sheer curtains, he would motion for me to come and sit near him. I would sit on the steps of the small platform. He would continue his conversations with the individual, without ever breaking his stride. I did not understand what was being said. I assumed it concerned a special privilege that the individual needed or concerned business of another Jains monastery.

I would eventually tiptoe out and silently wave good-bye. He would acknowledge me with a nod, never breaking his stride in conversation. There seemed to be a connection between the two of us, even though we had never spoken a word to each other.

There were various groups from many parts of India on retreat at the monastery, as well as our group. While walking around one day, I stopped and started chatting with a group sitting together beneath a tree. They were very well dressed and appeared to be financially well off. I learned that they were all related to one another and were there on retreat. It was a family of three generations. A young girl spoke some English and was able to converse and translate our dialogue. We spoke for some time, laughing and talking about children, and discussing various places I had visited in India. They were curious about the United States and asked many questions about my children and me.

"How is America?" my young interpreter asked.

"I do not live in a city but in the country. Every part of America is different, like your India."

"Do you have children?" my young friend asked.

"Yes, I have two children, a boy who is twenty and a daughter who is eighteen. She is attending a university."

"What are some of your favorite places that you have visited in India?"

"Each place that we have visited is unique and has its own beauty. I could never choose a place that is my favorite because I have enjoyed and learned something in each location; although, I am looking forward to seeing the Taj."

"We have been there. It is beautiful. It is one of the most famous places to visit in all of India. You will like seeing the Taj."

"The Taj is like our Statue of Liberty. Most foreigners who visit our country want to see it, just like your Taj. Do you know of the Statue of Liberty?"

"Yes, we read about it in books. None of us has been to America. I would like to visit it one day."

"I hope you do and I hope that your experience is as wonderful as mine has been in India."

Before parting, we each took pictures of each other and wished each other a life journey of peace and happiness. The grandfather, who had been silent all this time, surprised me by stating that he had something to say.

My young friend interpreted. "Please tell her that I have never met an American before, but I hope that all Americans are like her."

My interaction with them had given them a perspective of Americans. I understood that in many ways, my fellow travelers and I were little ambassadors of America. Our actions and behavior in India reflected on all Americans.

In many ways, we had connected as human beings. His message was simple; we had loved and respected each other for a brief moment, for the core of who we are, not for the expectations we place on each other because of religious affiliation or country of birth. His voice, face, and significant insight have reverberated in my heart many times throughout my life since.

While we were at the monastery, my fellow travelers and I were to write a paper on a topic of our choice based on our studies in India. I chose to write about the simplicity and core connection that all religions have. Our group had studied and discussed the various religions of the East: Islam, Jainism, Buddhism, and Hinduism. The central theme of my paper reflected upon the two following paragraphs.

"The thread that connects all religions is the fact that it leads to the same source, same Truth, same God. No matter what we call the source or in what language, the meanings are the same, Giver of Life, Eternal love, and All that Is.

The truths of all religions are the same—the sacredness of life, empathy for others, condemnation of violence, charity for the less fortunate, and the practice of virtue. It is only through man that the messages have been lost and the essence of Truth distorted."

I was amazed at the depth of the changes within me, to accept these statements. I was open to the life-lessons that were being presented before me.

Before we left, the head of the monastery bestowed special names on Professor Ashok, Professor Suzanne and me. The name he bestowed upon me translated to mean "Searcher of Truth". It was an insightful name and was rather startling that he had connected that name to me. His special name for me made me stop and think. He had put into words what I needed to acknowledge within myself.

I meditated and prayed at many temples during my time in India, and felt a sense of freedom and peace in all of them. Without my realizing it, I had acknowledged all religions and accepted them all as one. I did not impose my expectations but accepted the differences. Because of this inner revelation, I had been able to find the peace and connection to the various rituals, chants, and people.

THE WEDDING

It was the second week in November by now and our travel was soon ending. Professor Ashok said that it was time to have some fun after all the work and studying we had done. His nephew was getting married not far from where we were. The final wedding festivities were deliberately delayed so our group could attend.

We dropped our luggage in the hotel, where the final wedding celebration was taking place the next day. We went to the groom's home to meet him and Professor Ashok's family.

The home was beautiful and spacious. There were large bedrooms with real bedding and other living quarters. The home had an indoor toilet and running water. There was a wonderful large eat-in kitchen.

The house surrounded a courtyard. Servants scurried around and provided beverages for our group. The young handsome groom was dressed in a light gray suit. He was of medium build with dark hair, flashing dark eyes, and a very thick mustache. He sat in the middle of the courtyard surrounded by his family. White sheets were spread on the ground and cushions placed for us to sit.

A garland of flowers made of marigolds was placed around the neck of the groom. Family members were coming up to the young man and smearing him with some kind of paste, which I later learned was a mixture of turmeric, rosewater, and sandalwood. I was encouraged to do the same. I had a hard time smearing his head and face and gently rubbed it; they laughed at me.

I asked Bipina, "Do the females have the same kind of pre-wedding rituals that the males have?"

"Yes, most of them are the same, such as the smearing of the turmeric paste. This is to purify the body before embarking on matrimony. The pre-wedding rituals are as important as the wedding ceremony in the Hindu religion. One of the rituals that the males do not have is a mehndi party. The bride-to-be will gather her female friends and female family members to decorate each other's hands and feet with henna designs, or they might bring in a professional."

"That sounds like a lot of fun," I said.

"Yea it really is. Of course, the hands and feet of the bride-to-be will have the most elaborate designs. The darker and more elaborate her hands and feet are the more good luck it will bring. This also, signifies that her mother-in-law loves her."

"I bet the older females will give some funny advice to the bride-to-be at the henna party."

"That's part of the fun. It is also the last few days before the wedding and the family is ready to have fun and relax after all the preparations for the wedding," Bipina said.

"Do the designs have significance?" I asked.

"Yes, they are intricate and are meant for good life and prosperity. For example, flower buds mean new life and love, and paisley symbols mean love, fertility, and good luck."

"I imagine that there must be a lot of conversation as to what needs to be designed with a lot of laughter."

"Oh yeah! A trick that most Indian brides do is to place the bridegroom's name or initials among the intricate designs. He is supposed to search for his name or initials."

"What happens if he doesn't find them?" I asked.

"It signifies that she will be dominating in the first seven years of marriage," Bipina said.

"I think that I would try very hard to make it absolutely impossible for him to find it."

"That's the idea," Bipina said.

"That's a neat tradition," I said.

"Yes and the bride-to-be cannot smear the henna before the wedding, so of course she cannot do any housework, and is therefore waited upon," Bipina said.

"Now I really like this tradition."

"Also, when she moves in with her husband's family, she is not to do any work there either, until the henna wears off."

"Ok, I think I would find a way to extend this tradition," I said.

"They do, they rub lemon juice to preserve the design."

"Now that's a smart woman," I said.

The pre-wedding party was still going on when our group left the young man's home. I was exhausted after the long bus trip. The group chatted away on the bus getting back to our hotel.

The morning of the wedding, Bipina, Heather, Maegan, Esmahan, Jen, and I were in and out of each other's rooms, laughing, giggling, and helping to dress one another in our new Indian clothing. The girls had all bought saris. I had chosen a gold silk sari with red trim. The young men, Patrick, Luke, John, and Aaron had bought dhotis to wear. Amber left for home a few days before the wedding.

Watching each other walk in the new Indian clothing was hysterical. Having spent so much time together, experiencing all that we had, there was a strong bond among us.

Early evening, on the day of the wedding, our group arrived at the groom's home energized with the anticipation of what was before us. The handsome groom was dressed in a white long jacket and matching pants. A white turban was on his head and trimmed in red. I later learned that the color red had significant meaning; good luck being one of them.

A white horse arrived, also decorated in red trim. The groom promptly got on the horse. A small child of about four, dressed in a silk silvery suit, was handed to him. Four men lifted a canopy on poles, adorned with marigold flowers. They carried the canopy over the groom, the child, and the horse. The band started playing.

Guests of the groom started dancing in the streets, following the band and the groom to the hotel where the bride, her family, and friends, were waiting for us to arrive. Lit lanterns all strung up together on each side of the wedding party lighted the way. At one point, we passed another wedding party on the opposite side, dancing to their destination as well. A man teasingly gestured for me to join their party. The festivities of dancing, singing, and yelling grew even louder, as each wedding party tried to outdo the other. Everyone was having so much fun and there was so much laughter and joy. My fellow travelers and I were exuberant. This was a normal custom for the Indian people and it was exciting and thrilling for our group to be a part of it. It seemed that we danced for miles before we reached the hotel. I wore out my heels on the stone dirt road and was never able to wear them again.

When we arrived at the hotel, the bride's family was waiting for us at the entrance. The shy bride was dressed in a bright red sari with gold trim. A red sheer veil, also outlined in gold, was draped over her long dark hair. The young bride was in her late teens. She was slender and of medium height. Her dark eyes were outlined in black, which enhanced her beauty. She wore the traditional nose ring. Her skin was flawless. She was stunning. She was adorned with gold jewelry. Gold jewelry is auspicious so the more they wear, the more good luck and happiness they will have. *She will have lots of happiness.*

I was anxious to look at her hands and feet and view the henna designs. They were intricate and very dark. I wondered where she had hidden the grooms name or initials.

The bride and groom exchanged leis of marigolds at the entryway of the hotel. This exchange is symbolic of accepting one another. The bride's parents stood on each side of her, smiling and ready to welcome the groom's family. The groom's immediate family and I were adorned with leis of marigold flowers.

A punch bowl was waiting for the dancing guests. We were all thirsty and everyone rushed to it. The punch had a sweet flavor of coconut.

The Brahmin priest went around the bride and groom saying mantras. The bride and groom interacted with the priest. Everyone sat down to a delicious buffet of vegetables, rice, samosa, and Naan bread, which I had come to love. Some sweet delicacies were there as well. The bride and groom sat together at their own table in front of their guests. They exchanged shy smiles and fed each other a forkful of food.

After dinner, the young couple was escorted to a flower-decorated stage, where they sat for the rest of the evening. Guests took turns going up and offering their good wishes to the young couple. I was no exception.

Everyone left, the wedding was over, or so I thought. Later, as soon as I had fallen asleep, I was awakened by a light knock on the door. A young man was at the doorway, which I recognized as a member of the groom's family. He gestured for me to go with him. Quietly I dressed in the dark and followed him. I was amazed that we went to the rooftop of the hotel.

The immediate family of the bride and groom were waiting for me. They were excited to see me and had a cushion waiting for me to sit among them. They had chosen me to share, in what I soon realized, was the actual wedding ritual.

There was a large white canopy with billowy curtains flowing all around. The bride and groom sat under a flowered canopy, which was inside the white canopy. The flowered canopy was the same one that the groom had ridden under, on the way to the hotel. The groom's parents presented the bride with jewelry. The bride's parents presented the groom with presents as well. A small fire was lit. I later learned that fire is regarded as a purifying element in Hindu rituals. The young couple recited mantras along with their religious leader. Then the bride and groom circled the fire holding hands saying mantras. Rituals were performed and crowns of flowers were placed on the bride and groom. The bride and groom then exchanged their garlands. The groom gave his young shy bride his hand. His sash was tied to her sari; they were just united in marriage. The bride and groom circled the fire led by the Brahmin priest. The bride took the lead the first three times and the groom took the lead during the last four times. This, I was later informed, symbolizes who will take the lead during the first seven years of marriage. I found this rather interesting that the woman should be first. The rituals took a while, as there were different stages to the ceremony.   There was no one to translate but I did not need any explanations as to what was to follow. I understood that it was time for the bride and groom to leave. It was an emotional moment as the bride's parents grasped their daughter in their arms and cried. There was, however, a light moment as someone said something and all turned, looked at me, and laughed. Tears were flowing down my cheeks at witnessing this universal moment. I tried to hide behind a very thin pole. The young couple was then escorted by the new husband's family and into a waiting car.

There would be other rituals when the young couple arrived at the home of the groom. They would play games to introduce her to her new family. Even though this young bride is to be subservient to her mother-in-law, she was going to a wonderful family where hardship would be minimal. The family had prepared a servant, a girl of about ten, to meet the bride's needs.

The wedding was a beautiful experience and I felt honored to have witnessed this very special and sacred event. Even though I had gone to many weddings in the past, this wedding would always remain as a very special memory. I had been personally engaged and not a spectator. I had been in the moment and had shared in the connection of the sacred event. I would never view weddings in the same nonchalant way. I had to go half way around the world to appreciate the richness and beauty of something that I had viewed as an ordinary event. It is far from being ordinary, but extraordinary and a beautiful cycle of life. The following morning as I was packing, I heard Heather, another fellow traveler, exclaim as she was looking out the window, "Oh my God!" I ran to the window to see what she was looking at. Across the street below was a naked man covered in ashes from head to toe. This man had given away his worldly possessions to achieve favor with God. In our studies, we had learned that some religions in India, in one form or another, believe this practice. The belief is to release the soul from bondage to the body in order to unite with God. The idea seemed absurd, but having had time since to think about this, I have come to realize that it is also part of the Christian religion, called penance. If one does something with deep belief, then who am I to say that what that man does is shocking.

We went to the groom's home the next day to say our farewells to the family and found the young newlyweds being entertained by female dancers. I noticed that the dancers looked different, not the usual shy Indian women I had been accustomed to seeing. They were elaborately made-up and had on colorful clothing, bright pink saris. I was informed they were eunuchs and made a living by performing fertility dances for newlyweds. The eunuchs knew who was getting married and which families could afford to pay them. They would show up at the groom's home the day after the wedding and perform their dances. It would have been bad luck to turn them away.

The eunuchs were dancing, singing, and banging on tambourines. "I do not believe that India has a fertility problem," I said to Meagan. Making sure I was not jinxing the young couple, I joined in the dancing and laughter.

I have come to realize that I had not turned away from the differences of people. I was acknowledging and celebrating the uniqueness of humankind. The essence of All is the same in everyone. All are part of All that is. The essence of love, loves us all equally and unconditionally.

TAJ MAHAL

Our time in India was almost over; it was the middle of November and we only had a week left. Every day was exciting and memorable. I tried to savor each new experience as they unfolded before me. We studied in class the history of the place we were to visit and then the next day we would experience the authenticity and flavor of the location. I became aware that this was a one-of-a-kind experience and that I was on an extraordinary journey, on many levels. These facts amazed me and never left me. I would think, "How many people at my age, with two teenage kids, have the opportunity to have this kind of adventure?" If my camera was not clicking away, my mind was capturing every nuance of the event.

On our travels we visited many temples, castles, and museums. The Taj Mahal or as it is lovingly called, The Taj, was the most anticipated location.

We left to see The Taj at dawn. The roads that led us to The Taj were bumpy dirt roads littered with shacks, representative of the poverty in India. Beggars were waiting outside the gate of The Taj, even though it was early morning.

To reach The Taj I had to walk through various archways that seemed to frame the building's distinctive architectural features. With each archway I walked through, The Taj appeared to be getting larger and larger. Eventually, the last arch I walked through opened onto a large terrace with a courtyard below. I was finally looking at The Taj, directly in front of me on the opposite platform. The morning sky was radiating on The Taj with various hues of blue and pink. The distinctive shape of The Taj stood out in the morning sky and seemed to transform with the glistening colors that it absorbed. Suddenly the colors faded and The Taj became a brilliant, glistening white in the deep blue sky. It astounded me. I was spell bound. This was a surreal moment. It was as though I was looking at a postcard. It was large and majestic!

I could not rush to The Taj like some of my fellow travelers. I stood there and breathed in the experience of what I was seeing. I kept saying, "Am I really looking at The Taj Mahal, one of the Seven Wonders of the World?" Bipina stood next to me in silence, smiling. She too seemed to have been struck with awe.

I was amazed with the reality of what I was feeling and seeing and said to Bipina, "How can such magnificence and beauty exist among the rubble around it? It's as though this is a symbol of hope and love in the midst of poverty and deprivation. It appears to be suspended out of nowhere and yet, it encompasses everywhere and everything."

Bipina looked at me with misty eyes, smiled and said, "I know what you mean." She too was experiencing an emotional moment.

The history of The Taj was presented to us as a love story, a display of love from a man to a woman. Here was the legend I had studied and was now looking at, in all its elegance and majesty.

Professor Ashok had informed us of the legend of The Taj Mahal. Queen Mumtaz was the second wife of the Emperor Shah Jahan. He had seen Mumtaz in the market place and asked his father for permission to marry her. He was not given permission because of protocol; instead he married the woman that had been chosen for him. Five years later he finally married Mumtaz. When Mumtaz was expecting their fourteenth child, eight of whom lived, she went out to the battlefield to be with her husband. When Shah Jahan was informed that Mumtaz was coming, he went to meet her and got lost. When he finally reached her, she was dying. She had given birth to a baby girl. On her deathbed, she asked him for one last wish, a display in memory of their love. Overcome with grief, Shah Jahan devoted the rest of his life to building her a mausoleum. It took twenty-two years to build the Taj which Shaw Jahan designed.

Even with its beauty and love story, I could not help but think that there was much more to the legend. The Taj Mahal is tinged with anguish, greed, and pain. Shah Jahan had four sons who battled for power of his kingdom. Shah Jahan was imprisoned the last eight years of his life, at the Red Fort, not far from where he supposedly could view The Taj Mahal being built from his cell. His last wish was to be buried alongside his wife, Mumtaz.

As I looked at The Taj, I reflected upon Princess Diana. Four years earlier, in 1992, she too had visited The Taj. The picture of the Princess sitting alone in front of The Taj Mahal, the greatest symbol of love, had resonated around the world. Newspapers made speculations about her marriage that I did not want to believe. It is now common knowledge that she desperately and hopelessly had tried to create happiness from a flawed foundation like Shah Jahan.

Along with millions of people, I too had gotten up in the middle of the night to watch the fairy tale story of a commoner who got her prince. Diana allowed us to believe that fairy tales do come true; it was to be shattered years later. In time, the world would know the isolation and pain she endured during her years of marriage to Prince Charles. She and I had both been entrapped in a perpetual nightmare. A week before our group left for India, Princess Diana was granted the divorce.

In time, Prince Charles, like Shah Jahan, married the woman he had wanted, even though royal protocol had tried to prevent it. Prince Charles and Shah Jahan are the ones whose fairy tale *did* come true in the end, I thought.

As I am recalling all these things, I wondered if I had become cynical about love. Had I given up the fact that there is no such thing as true love? No, I thought, there were reasons for being in those marriages. Princess Diana, as well as me, had reasons to be in a flawed marriage. Our purpose and journey in life would not begin until we came to the crossroads of divorce.

I wondered if Princess Diana had thought and felt many of the things that I was experiencing as I was looking at The Taj Mahal.

I was suddenly feeling lucky, elated, and grateful to be free of the burdens of my marriage. I never could have imagined that in three short years I would have these feelings, while looking at one of the Seven Wonders of the World. If I could get here in such a short time, from where I had been, then I could achieve anything, I thought.

I had not lost love; instead, I had found love within myself by giving it freely and unconditionally to the children I encountered in India. Here I was looking at the symbol of love. I understood the freedom and gift I had been given, the experience of unconditional love. In time, Princess Diana too seemed to have found her self-worth and love by helping others. My heart was full and overflowing with abundant joy.

I had viewed The Taj from every direction and angle from a distance. I had wanted to savor this moment. An hour had gone by and it was now time to view The Taj up close.

It sits on a high platform at the far end of the flower gardens and reflective pools. I started descending the steps of the platform from where I had been viewing the entire area. I walked around the raised walkways and the fragrant flower gardens of the manicured grounds. Another hour went by before I finally started going up the white marble stairs that led to the platform where The Taj Mahal stood. At the top of the stairs I turned. The Taj was behind me now. I looked at the flower gardens, the manicured grounds, and the fountains below me and realized that they were an empty reflection without the majesty of The Taj.

I looked up at the white glistening domes on top of the

mausoleum. The platform that the Taj sits on is wide with large white marble stones that have a brown design. On each side of the Taj there is a beautiful golden-brown marble building with small white domes on top. One of the buildings is a mosque and the other was built to keep the symmetry to The Taj.

I touched The Taj, it was real! I walked into the mausoleum where Shaw Jahan and Mumtaz were laid to rest. The tombs are on an elevated podium surrounded by an intricate lacy barrier made of marble. Shah Jahan's tomb is bigger than Mumtaz's. The tombs are a creamy pale peach color with intricate designs all around. There are various colorful flowers with green leaves etched in the marble on the upper level of the barrier and on the upper walls of the mausoleum. The room is octagonal with windows on top to allow the light to pass through the lacy marble. It was an amazing experience to have visited this wonder of the world.

I had absorbed all the beauty of The Taj. I started walking back through the gardens to join my group. A tune popped in my head and I started singing and laughing at myself, *"If they could see me now, that little gang of mine, la la la, da da da, they wouldn't believe it, if my friends could see me nowww."* I could not believe it either.

Upon my return, I wanted to learn more about The Taj Mahal and started doing some research. To my utter surprise and disappointment, I found various articles and books stating that Shah Jahan did not build the Taj Mahal. I did not want to believe this.

The books explained in great depth that Akbar the Great Mogul, who preceded Shah Jahan by one hundred years, actually built The Taj Mahal. One of these authors and historians is P.N. Oak who wrote, Tajmahal: The True Story, published by A. Gosh. He goes on to explain that The Taj had been an ancient Hindu temple for Shiva known as Tejo Mahalaya.

I was able to contact V. S. Godbole, an author who also disputes that Shah Jahan built the Taj Mahal. His books include—Concerning This Great Lie—Simple Analysis of a Great Deception (2nd edition 2007), Taj Mahal and the Great British Conspiracy (1996).

In our correspondence, I asked V. S. Godbole as to why this fabrication was allowed to continue when there is evidence that Shah Jahan did not build The Taj Mahal. His reply was, "When people realize that The Taj Mahal was not built by Shah Jahan, they then ask—why does it matter? I have answered the question in my booklet—Why Rewrite Indian History. It explains why both the Indian government and Indian Historians have ducked the issue."

There is truth to his statement and I believe that it goes much deeper. The lie will continue because people have the desire to want to believe in the fairy tale love story.

THE CREMATION

The last week of our trip was spent at a beach resort in a small fishing village called Mahablieporium. When my fellow travelers and I arrived and saw the beach, we dropped our luggage in the lobby and ran towards the ocean. It was the first familiar thing we had seen in months. We jumped in the water with our clothes on and playfully started pushing and splashing one another. We must have looked like lunatics. It was such an incredible and refreshing feeling. Here I thought, we will be away from the poverty and the chaos that we have experienced for the past three months. Except for a few huts on the beach, it appeared that the hotel was the only thing in the area. How wrong could I be?

I spent a great deal of time walking the beach and reflecting on the trip and my life. At one point, I questioned Professor Ashok concerning the accomplishments, especially starting the school. I still wondered if a one-room schoolhouse could be why God had sent me halfway around the world. It does not seem much compared to the personal transformation I had to go through, I thought.

"It's not a school that we started. It is only a classroom," I said to Professor Ashok.

In his great wisdom he replied, "It is only the beginning. It has the possibility to grow."

"What about the money to keep it going? How can I continue raising money? The school has only enough money for the next three years," I said.

"We will find a way," he stated.

I was already carrying the burden of the school before I even left India.

One day I was walking the beach and came upon a small village which was beyond a sand dune. I walked among a maze of straw huts. It was apparent there was no electricity, no running water, and nothing but deprivation. Everyone seemed to know that there was an intruder and poked their heads out of their huts. I was moved of course, by the simplicity and the poverty. A young woman who did not speak English conversed with hand signals. I understood what she was saying, "Help us."

I did not know what to say, so I said, "Someday I will return."

She nodded as if to say, "I understand." I can still see her eyes and face pleading. Every so often I recall that promise.

Fishing was the livelihood of the village. One morning I saw a group of men pushing a fishing boat from the beach into the water. I stopped to help them push the boat. They stopped and a man gently took my hands off the boat. They have pride, I thought, or maybe it is bad luck to have a woman push, or possibly both. I never found out.

The day before we were leaving the seaside and India, I prepared for a walk. I hesitated whether I should take the camera. The camera had become an extension of my hand as I had tried to capture and savor the moments of my experiences. "How can there possibly be anything that I haven't already taken a picture of," I said loudly to myself. I left the camera in the room.

I was half way down the beach when suddenly I heard the faint familiar sound in the distance of what I had come to call a procession for the dead. I could see in the distance numerous people walking towards me. There was the familiar sight and sound of a few trumpet players. Following was the body of the deceased, covered with the pungent, orange flowers of marigolds. This was being carried on a board on the shoulders of several men.

For a moment, I stood there frozen and mesmerized, watching them walk toward me, as the music got louder and louder.

I quickly turned and ran back to the hotel room. I grabbed my camera and ran back down the beach. I suddenly stopped. I looked up and down the beach but did not see the procession anywhere, nor did I hear the sound of the trumpet players. Where in the world did they go, I asked myself as I twirled around looking. There were a few people on the beach; realizing my dilemma, and without saying a word, they all pointed in the same direction, over a sand dune. I looked in the direction they were pointing and noticed a trail of orange flowers. I followed the path to where the flowers led me.

As I walked over the sand dune, directly before me, was a sight that has been etched in my mind forever. I understood that a body was being prepared for cremation. I stood still not knowing what to do. The group of people stopped, looked at me, but did not gesture for me to leave, which was unusual. What's more unusual, I did not turn around and run.

I pointed at my camera and hand signaled whether I could take pictures. They looked at one another and mumbled amongst each other. A young man who was leaning over the body nodded his head as if to say, yes. I immediately started photographing what was before me.

The young man started pushing the flowers off the body, revealing a very frail, thin, old woman. Her hair was pulled back, not yet very gray, but she looked about one hundred years old. She had on a long dark blue dress. She was barefoot of course. The young man started taking off her jewelry, first her rings and then bracelets. He gently and lovingly folded the frail hands one over the other. He stopped and waited for me to take pictures as I hobbled around. In my eagerness to grab the camera, I had not taken the time to put on shoes. There were sharp stones and thorns around. A very thin, little old man, who was scantily dressed, realized my dilemma, pointed towards his flip-flops and gestured. He loaned me one of his most valuable possessions. I was grateful to him as I slipped them on.

The body was laid out on flat bamboo planks, suspended above a pile of wood. I watched as they covered the body with dry cow patties. I noticed that the soles of the deceased's feet were not covered. They told a story of hardship. The fire was started underneath the body and on the cow patties above. The young man, who may have been her son, and the one who had nodded allowing me to take pictures, was scantily dressed in a dhoti with a bare chest. He hoisted a large clay jug on one shoulder. Another man stood behind him, holding the jug steady with one hand and a hammer type object in the other. Rituals were being chanted, as the two men walked around the body. The man with the hammer would periodically hit the jug and water would spill over the bare-chested young man.

This went on until all the water had spilled out of the jug. Meanwhile, the body was burning. It was dusk by this time. The flames were leaping in the dark. I stopped photographing. I could see a group of men, squatting on the far side, passing a pipe among each other. Women and men stood silently together around the burning body and watched the flames leap in the dark.

I later learned that only men were allowed to attend to the body and prepare it for cremation. Usually the eldest son or a close male family member, who would become head of the household, would take part in the actual ceremony. Mustaches for men were highly prized in India and it seemed that most men had a mustache. This is a sign of virility and manhood; yet, this had to be shaved off and nails cut short to take part in the cremation ceremony. Only family members were allowed to witness the cremation and women were usually discouraged to attend. No emotions of sadness were to be expressed, the belief being that the soul is considered to still be present to view the loved ones they are leaving behind. The showing of emotion would hamper the deceased from leaving.

As I looked at the body, many thoughts wandered in my mind. What kind of life has this woman led? From her surroundings and the conditions of her feet, she must have had many hardships. I was seeing death in a different perspective than I had ever thought about before. I believed that this was not the end for her but the beginning of a new life on a spiritual level where there will be no pain or hardships, only love and new adventures. There will be no status or divisions, but equality in the presence of the Divine. No one can bring his or her attachments or accumulations of riches from earth. The only thing we take is the love we have given and the love we have received. Love never dies.

My belief is that her body is only a casing that holds her essence, her truth, which slipped out with the last breath she exhaled. She would be amused at watching her body burning and seeing me amongst her family. She probably would understand the mystery of why I am there, better than I do. The departed loved ones, who have been waiting for her to cross over, are along her side, reassuring her that everything will be fine.

She probably would be sad and emotional, because of not being able to share in the everyday lives of the loved ones she is leaving behind. It would be apparent that if she could come back, even with the hard life she has led, she could justify her reasons to want to be with her family. Not many people are ever ready to leave this earth for something we do not know about. Those who are waiting next to her will gently escort her to the exciting new life that is awaiting her. She will enter a new existence beyond her wildest imagination.

My belief is that she will come back from time to time to see how the family she left behind is evolving. She will be able to connect with them in their hearts and souls because her essence will touch them there, as a reminder of her presence. She will become frustrated because she will not be able to speak to them and in time will move on and come back less and less. I began to look at death for what it is, beauty and the promise that it holds.

I looked down and noticed something shiny in the dark. I picked it up and did not know what to do with it. Without thinking or realizing what I was doing, I tossed the coin on top of the body. Everyone gasped; I was mortified. 'Oh my God, what have I done?' It was later that I was informed that it was auspicious, a good luck gesture. Their belief is that I had given money to the deceased woman for her journey home.

It was time for me to leave them to their privacy. I silently stepped back, turned, and walked away. It was dark with only the moon shining on the ocean and the light from the hotel at the far end of the beach. I could hear the ripples of the waves as they gently hit the shore. I was aimlessly walking on the beach, lost in thoughts, when I felt that someone was following me. I quickly spun around ready to face my intruder. At once, I recognized the stature of the little old man who had loaned me his flip-flops. I had forgotten that I was still wearing them. I was laughing at myself, at the thought of that poor man following behind me. I quickly and silently slipped out of them, and he slipped into them. I did not know how to express my gratitude so I bowed. He shyly bowed back. He then silently turned, walked away and was engulfed in the darkness. He will never know how many times in my life I have thought of him and thanked him from my heart.

I continued my walk, barefoot, in the soft cool sand. I had time to ponder my experiences and the irony of the shoes, during my last moments in a country and people that touched me deeply. For three months, I had felt that I had walked in their shoes and the time had come for me to slip out of them. Somehow, I had felt the pain they experienced. I had shared in their simple joy of being in the moment. It was only by experiencing all these things, that I could accept the cremation and not find it offensive, repugnant, or morbid. Death is another facet of life and the continuation of the soul to another level. Incredible to say, it was my last day in India and I had experienced the last facet of the life cycle. I had witnessed birth, participated in the marriage ritual, and now completed the cycle with the viewing of the death ritual. India had something to teach me even at the last moment; the humbleness and simplicity of death.

In a strange land with different languages and cultures, the people of India and I had transgressed the multitude of differences that separate us. My soul was overflowing with love; my restlessness, hunger, and thirst were gone. All my tears had been turned to joy, all these things and more, I knew.

"What an incredible mountain I have climbed," I whispered to the Indian Ocean. "It is now time for me to come down the mountain, slip out of your life and country, and slip back to mine."

On the train to Varanasi. Me, Heather,
Aaron, Esmahan, John, & Luke.

Little girl looking for food
in the garbage across from
our hotel in Varanasi.

Entrepreneurs setting up
shop in the streets.

Taj Mahal.

On the train with my fellow travelers. Bipina,
Maegan, Patrick, Jen, Heather, & me.

Life in the streets.

The older woman holding her husband's love-child, with
her two daughters. This is where they ate and slept.

Two sisters searching in the garbage for food.

Woman making cow patties.

Shoe repairman on a New Delhi street.

Amber and me at the Spastic Society.

The little children who stole my heart.

Bipina, me, Professor Suzanne, and a very happy Indian.

Our group on an excursion in Jaipur. Bipina, Patrick, Heather, Amber, Jen, Luke, me, & Maegan in front.

Queen Jean, me, Princess Ganga, & Esmahan.

Our group at the castle in Dundlod.

Brick housing for travelers built by our group
& local community members.

Prince Bonnie & Princess Ganga.

First day of school at the Indo-International School.

Outside of the Indo-International School.

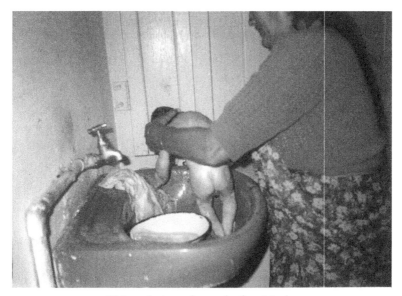

Shirag being cleaned after birth.

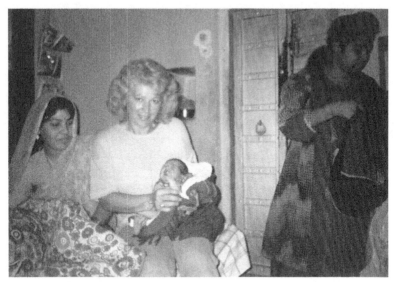

Shirag, me, and his mother the day after his birth.

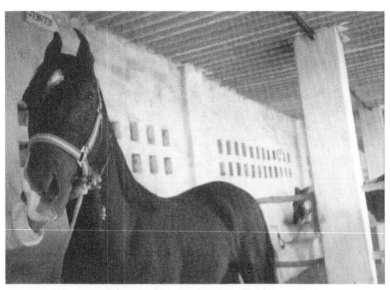

Mawari horse at Prince Bonnie's stables.

Riding a camel to King Rex's house.

Children teaching me to carry a pot on my head.

The family of three generations at the Jain Monastery.

Jain monks.

At the wedding with Professor Suzanne, me, Luke, & Aaron.

At the Jain Monastery with some very happy young visitors.

The happy wedding couple.

Relaxing together. Maegan, Patrick, Esmahan,
Heather, me, Bipina, & Jen.

Fisherman at Mahabalipuram.

Maegan, me & Heather.

Riding horses on the beach at Mumbai.

My buddy Aaron & me.

Preparing the body for cremation.

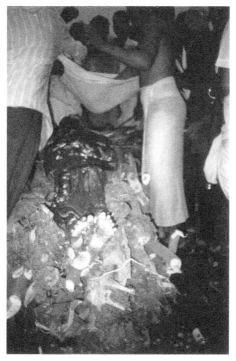

The feet on the body that tell a story.

The cremation ritual.

The last picture taken of our group together.

Section 3

A SMALL BODY OF DETERMINED SPIRITS
FIRED BY AN UNQUENCHABLE
FAITH IN THEIR MISSION
CAN ALTER THE COURSE OF HISTORY.

Mahatma Gandhi

THANKSGIVING DINNER

Ironically, we arrived in the United States a few days before Thanksgiving; a day of giving thanks for the bounty we have in our lives. Getting back to my surroundings and the abundance we have in this country was almost as painful to accept as the poverty I had left behind in India.

Going to the grocery story for the first time, after being in India for three months, was shocking. I was ridden with guilt at seeing the amount of food that was in the store. There are no grocery stores in India, only the vendors in the streets. I barely selected what I needed that day and left quickly, choking back tears. I had a hard time adjusting to having so much available to me, knowing that the children I left behind had so little.

Thanksgiving dinner was no exception. Mama and Papa's restaurant was closed and we had dinner there in order to accommodate the expanding family. The table was full of the usual Thanksgiving meal; turkey, sweet potatoes, stuffing and of course what my kids call Nonna's red dishes, such as lasagna, meatballs, and much more. I had a hard time swallowing as I was choking back tears.

I tried to enlighten my family about my experiences in India but it was impossible to put into words, both the deprivation and the joys, I experienced. Words could not convey my passion for the children of India. My brothers teased me and inquired if I was still Italian.

Many of the experiences in India flashed through my mind as everyone chatted away. India seemed a world away now. A few days ago I had witnessed a cremation and here I sat at a table laden with food that could probably feed that entire fishing village.

India and her people had infiltrated the depth of my soul. I was recalling the many faces and incidents I had left behind. I also missed my fellow travelers. I wondered how they were doing and if they were feeling as alienated as I was. We had been together every waking hour and now we were dispersed.

While in India, I would ask a different fellow traveler to spend time with me during my many walks or to sit with me on those long, slow, train rides. We would sit in the open train door and place our feet on the train steps. It always seemed that I could walk faster than the train was moving. I now could almost hear the clickety-clack of the train on the tracks, the long hollow sound of the whistle blowing, and the smell of the billowing smoke from the engine. I knew these were special moments that I had shared with my fellow travelers. I wanted them to see India through my eyes. I learned from them and they learned from me.

I recalled sitting with Bipina on the steps of the open train door while looking out at the countryside. Bipina was always ready to go for walks and translate when needed. She was petite with olive skin and long dark hair, tied in the back. Her ready smile was contagious. Her dark bright eyes were deep and reflective. I had a connection with Bipina. I understood that her experience was unique. Like me she had come to America as a child and she was in India searching to connect with her roots.

Our group had traveled in the northern part of India. There was little variety there to the villages. The countryside was barren with little to no vegetation. There were sparse communities scattered along the train tracks with many straw or cow-patty huts. We saw children attending schools under trees. We could see women carrying large baskets on their heads. It was amazing how they kept their balance. We saw women washing clothes in the streams with clothes spread out on the ground to dry.

One view that I will never forget is the morning rituals that

I witnessed. I could see villages in the far distance and men squatting in the fields close to the train, facing the track. I would wave at them and with their wide smiles, they would wave back. Later, I was informed that they went behind the village, into the fields for their morning rituals, to relieve themselves. I continued to wave and laugh at myself at the absurdity and yet, the simplicity of what I was observing.

At one point Bipina and I saw every mode of transportation in India, one following the other like a parade; the camel, the elephant, the rickshaw, the three-wheel motor vehicle, motorcycle and car. We had a good laugh together because only in India could we experience this.

Jennifer was tall, lanky, long dark haired, with introspective dark eyes. She had inner and outer beauty. I had a comfortable and peaceful feeling when I was with Jennifer. The pain of the poverty we encountered reflected in her eyes.

Meagan was beautiful in every way. She was fair with the prettiest rosy cheeks and beautiful blue eyes. Her short hair framed her round face. We were from the same university and our friendship continued after our trip. We would get together and make big pots of diet cabbage soup in my kitchen. She thought she was fat, which of course, she was not.

Esmahan was petite and had a unique appearance. She looked like a beautiful gypsy with her long dark cascade of curls, big bright almond eyes, and quick smile. She wore those long Indian dresses as though she had always worn them.

Amber, our California blond-haired girl, was very quiet and determined. She and I had shared the unique experience of being together at the Spastic Society in New Delhi. Her patience with feeding the children amazed me.

Sweet Heather was just a bundle of joy and excitement. She was petite, slender, and tan. Her long auburn hair framed her beautiful face. She was very athletic and ready for any adventure. I recalled how she convinced Megan and me to walk over to a neighboring hotel to go swimming in their pool. The staff, I am sure, knew we were not from that hotel but did not say anything. The girls provided entertainment for the staffers that afternoon with their playfulness in the pool.

Then there were the young men. Aaron was tall, with big shoulders. He had the widest smile I had ever seen. He was full of mischievousness. He had chosen to be my protector and companion on my many walks. A few years after we returned from India, I was informed that Aaron had died in a car accident. His death was painful for me.

John was shy and gentle and followed along with what the others had planned. He was of medium height and build. He and Luke seemed to be a throwback from the hippy era. They were both very down to earth.

Patrick was of slight build and had a quick smile under his beard. He seemed to be the coordinator of the many situations we got into, like the night we went drinking at the Taj Mahal hotel in New Delhi. The Indian beer is much stronger than our American beer.

Luke was tall with a medium build. He grew a beard while in India, which was very becoming. He had gotten accustomed to wearing the dhotis but he certainly did not blend in because of his fair skin and blue eyes. On one of our walks, we went by the Ashoka Hotel in New Delhi that was having a wedding reception. We were on the outside of the festivities looking in when a man from the wedding festivities came and escorted us to the bridal couple sitting on the podium. We became their honored guests, as they took pictures of us with the bridal couple. We were given platters of delicious food and were entertained by dancers and jugglers. It was rather amazing how cordial they were with us.

I felt that there was something deep and spiritual about Luke; he too seemed to have become absorbed in India. It was as though Luke was walking the walk with me whenever we spent time together. We would become subdued at what we were seeing and feeling, and there was not a need to discuss the moment. Luke left the group after Professor Ashok's nephew's wedding. He went on to see the camel races in Pushkar. Years later, we met again. Luke said that the camel races in Pushkar were a one-of-a kind experience. He said that he had gotten sick while he was there. An Indian family nursed him to health in their hut. He said that he would not be alive if it was not for the caring of those strangers. I recently heard that he is living in a commune somewhere in New York State. I have not been able to connect with him.

We had all shared a unique experience, and that will always be the connection in our lives. I believe that each of us were on this journey for a particular reason. I now wondered if they felt as I was feeling, as I sat with my family, isolated, sad, and alone.

I have often thought of my fellow travelers over the years and have wondered how their lives have turned out. How had India changed them? What reasons did they have to be on this trip? I have missed them and always will. There is, and always will be, a special place in my heart for each of them. I cannot help but smile with sadness and gratitude, whenever I think of them. They were there for me, as I had been there for them.

Here I was, surrounded with my family and yet, I was thinking of the many memories from the past few months. I was suddenly brought back to reality, as though an echo in my head was trying to get my attention, and heard Mama say, "Are you done with India now?" As a mother, I am sure she had been concerned for me.

No, my family would not and could not understand what I had experienced, nor could I share the depth of the anguish and joys that I held inside. I had to keep them bottled up, and accept the jabbing and teasing that my brothers made of my trip to India

THE RELUCTANT TRAVELER

In the meantime, I had to push India, the children, and my fellow travelers aside, and get on with my life; this was not an easy transition. Adjusting back to reality was emotional, but not as difficult as it had been to adjust to the reality of life in India. Still it was no small task. When I would run into Professor Suzanne, we would look at each other with an understanding half smile that said, "I know what you are feeling. I feel that way too."

I settled in to complete the last semester of my bachelor's degree in psychology at SUNY Oneonta. I was graduating that May. Louise was still upset that I had left her. In time, Louise would understand. For the moment I had to push that aside, because I had bigger problems that were haunting me.

I was carrying the burden of continuing the school I had left behind in India. I had not thought far ahead when the school was first started. Now it occurred to me that it was my responsibility, since I had brought the money that started the school. Questions after questions, with no answers in sight, were bombarding my waking hours: What's going to happen once the money runs out? How can I possibly continue with raising money? Family and friends are avoiding me when they see me coming; I do not blame them. Why had I not thought this far? What about the teachers? They are counting on the school to provide a living for their families. How are the children going to feel if the school closes?

It was a constant dilemma that I could not forget or let go. Something had to be done and I decided to go back to India to encourage the affluent Indian people from New Delhi to support the school we had started. I raised $2,000 by asking family and friends, and giving speeches at various organizations such as the Elks Club and Kiwanis.

My divorce from William had not been settled. By this time we had been separated about four years. The house disbursement was a dilemma and William continued on changing attorneys. I started receiving friendly phone calls from him. We chatted away as though the last four years of our lives, battling in the divorce courts, had never happened. One day he left a phone message saying, "Happy Anniversary". It was May 23, the anniversary date of when we met.

Louise and Albert heard the phone message. I was finishing packing for my flight the following morning to India, when both of them confronted me. Albert said very calmly, "Mom why is Papa leaving messages to you? Are you thinking of getting back with him?"

Louise stated, "Mom, Papa treated you bad before; do you think he is going to treat you better if he comes back?"

"If he returns, I am leaving," Albert said.

I knew they were right and there was only one thing to do. Early morning the following day, I called William's office and left him a phone message. "We no longer have anniversaries. Four years ago, I informed you that the back door was unlocked and that the light would be on for one year. You informed me to lock the door and stop wasting electricity. The door is now locked and the light is off."

Albert drove me to Kennedy Airport and that evening I took the flight to New Delhi. Here I was, the reluctant traveler going back, only this time completely alone. I had arranged with Prahn in New Delhi to set up speaking engagements. I arrived early morning the following day and was scheduled to speak that evening.

Prahn and his chauffeur picked me up to bring me to the scheduled speaking engagement. Prahn said, "There are about four hundred people that usually attend this meeting at the Ashoka Hotel. In the group are top officials from Parliament, affluent executives, and women, from all over India. Since they are educated, most of them understand and speak English." He also said, "The group continues to chat when the guest speakers speak, so don't be offended; this is their custom."

Prahn and I sat on a platform along with other officials. There was a guest speaker scheduled before me, a doctor, discussing in English, medicine and diseases in India. As Prahn had stated, the group continued to chat during his speech, which sounded like low humming. I looked around me and it appeared as though no one was listening to him. Oh God, I thought, what if no one listens to me either.

After Prahn introduced me, I stood up and walked over to the podium. I felt my knees buckle and I grabbed the podium with both hands. I have to make them understand that my mission has to be taken over, I thought. I gained strength from that reflection. The following are excerpts from the speech that was printed in their newsletter, along with my picture. The title of my speech was, '*One Village at a Time.*'

'I come here tonight to tell you of my dream and hope that by the time I leave here, you too will share my vision.

A year ago in May, I decided to enroll in the State University of New York's semester in India program. Little did I know the impact this decision would have on the lives of the people that I would touch. I only knew I had to come to India. Once the decision was made, being a non-traditional student and a mother of two grown children, my first thought was, what about the children of India? Will I be able to turn away when I feel their hunger and pain? I immediately knew the answers to these questions, and the immediate solution for me at the time seemed that I must raise money for the children of India. The generous contributions went a long way to accomplish many projects, one of them being starting an elementary school in a small town of Dundlod in the state of Rajasthan. From the various projects we undertook, we touched many lives. The Indian people and the children also touched me very deeply . . . .

To touch so many lives has been a humbling experience. I've come to realize that with this kind of commitment, comes responsibilities. I realized that I would have to devote my life to raising money every year, for the continuation of the school, unless I found an alternative solution. I had to come back to India not as a student but as a mother, an American woman, and ask for your help . . . .

I have also come to realize that one cannot fix everything all at once; however, if one can concentrate on 'one village at a time,' such a goal can become a reality. I recall hearing a story of a father and a son walking on the beach and came upon many starfish that were stranded on the shore. The son started to pick them up and throw them

back into the ocean. The father asked his son, 'Son, what difference does it make? There are so many of them.' The son replied, 'But Dad it makes a difference to this one,' as he threw a starfish into the ocean . . . .

Gandhiji, Bapuji was the greatest man that ever lived. Gandhiji had many dreams and many visions. Obtaining freedom for India was only the beginning. His desire and dream that every community in India be self-sufficient died with him. His children are still not free from hunger and pain . . . . One of the most powerful tools one can give to a child is an education that will provide training and skills. Education can elevate the poorest of the poor and the most oppressed individuals. It is not enough to educate the poor but it is the beginning. The challenge I offer you tonight is to adopt a community. All facets of that community must be embraced, such as housing, sanitation, safe water, health care, and of course education. Extend and reach, the return is a better future for India. The failure of not reaching out is the failure of the next generation. Put children first, not just your children, but all children. The spirit of giving must begin with you. The goal is to make the village of Dundlod, in the District of Jhunjhunu Rajasthan, a model community and once that is accomplished, we can follow that example to help other communities in India. I believe this can be accomplished when the people of India combine their energy, their talents, and their love towards this common goal of 'One Village at a Time'. . . .

There is an American saying, 'Give a man a fish and he will eat for the day, but teach him how to fish and he will eat for a lifetime.' If Bapuji were alive, it would be him addressing you on these issues . . . .

Gandhiji died ten months before I was born; yet I feel that I have known him all my life. I feel his pain and compassion when I walk among the poor. Nothing can be accomplished unless there is a beginning. It takes one person to have a dream, but it takes a group of people to make that dream become a reality. I have nothing to gain by being here tonight other than to quench this burning desire that I have for the children of India.' . . . .

The audience was quiet from the moment I began until the last word I spoke. At first no one moved as I finished. We looked at each other and then there was thunderous applause. They gave me a standing ovation. I had done all I could and had poured my heart to them.

In my speech, I also discussed the plight of building the first residential home and school for the disabled children in New Delhi. I told them the story of the two young sisters and the struggles the mother had in establishing a permanent home for them. She was in the audience. "What is going to happen to these children once the parents die?" I asked the politicians, executives, and women in the audience. After my speech I introduced her and she discussed her goals for the school. She was in tears by the time she finished speaking. The group of people immediately voted and took up the project of the school for the disabled. Years later, I was informed that the school for the disabled children had been built near New Delhi Airport.

I befriended a woman, Chandrika, who was at the meeting

and a member of parliament. "I don't know if anyone really heard my plea," I said to her.

"Relax, Jozee, you have planted a good seed. It takes time for the Indian people to work on things, but they heard you." Oh, how I wanted to believe her. Years would pass before I would know the answer.

We spent a few days together while I was in New Delhi. She took me to see the parliament buildings. Her chauffeur drove us around. She lived in an amazingly beautiful apartment, very American. She was very wealthy and proud to show me, and rightfully so. Her chauffeur lived, literally, in a closet outside her apartment door. There was only room for a very small cot. There was no door; he stepped onto the cot from the doorway. He attended to her needs.

There is a gulf between the rich and the poor in India, I thought. The rich get richer and the poor stay poor. The inequality of the rich and poor is not only in India but also in many parts of the world. The chauffeur, I am sure, must have felt fortunate to be employed, when so many are unemployed. The rich take advantage of poor people like him, because there are millions of people who would be ready to take his job.

Her chauffeur drove us to an area of New Delhi that I had never seen. I saw men, women, and children walking around holding hands. The women were all beautifully dressed with their bright blue and red saris. Their hair was coiffed perfectly. The men, with their slicked black hair and trimmed mustaches, strutted around with their families, dressed in creamy white loose trousers and shirts. The children wore shoes. These children do not go out in the streets begging or out in garbage piles looking for food, I thought. I had never seen this aspect of India. This is the way all of India should be, I said to myself.

I walked the streets of New Delhi and visited many of the places that the group and I had seen on our trip. I had been missing my fellow travelers and now even more so that I had returned to India. Even though we had been together in India seven months ago, it seemed a lifetime away.

I was anxious to visit Raj Ghat, on the banks of river Yamuna, where Gandhi's shrine and memorial rests. Gandhi, the father of India, was a Hindu. He had peacefully demonstrated against the British people to attain India's freedom. He was killed on January 30, 1948, and cremated the next day on the spot where he is now memorialized. Soon after his death, India attained its freedom from the British.

I bought a bouquet of flowers from the street vendor to bring to Gandhi's shrine. I walked the stone path in a manicured garden filled with flowers, fountains, and waterfalls that led to Gandhi's memorial site. I could see from the distance the large shiny black slab of marble. It was simple, elegant, and magnificent.

I placed the bouquet on top of the slab. I felt a connection with him and knew that I had done what he would have done, if he had been in my shoes. I walked around the grounds and kept talking to Gandhi about his India. I thought about how he had given his life for the greater good of others. I felt peacefulness, and completeness surrounding me. This was a strange and wonderful feeling and I had no idea why I had this feeling.

I had no idea where I was going the following fall. I had filled out an application at the University of Albany to continue my studies in psychology to work towards becoming a therapist. I was concerned about the traveling back and forth to Albany which was an hour away from home. A psychology degree did not go very far, a master's degree was needed. I had not heard from Albany University before I left for India, or so I thought. While walking the streets of New Delhi, the idea came to me to continue my studies in school counseling at the same university in Oneonta at home. I wondered why I had never thought of this before. I now had a new direction in my life.

I flew to Jaipur from New Delhi. Princess Ganga picked me up at the airport and we took a taxi to the castle. When I arrived there, I quickly dropped my luggage and went straight to the highest terrace, where our group and I had congregated. It felt empty without them. It was quiet. I thought of all the fun and laughter my fellow travelers and I had shared just seven months earlier. I looked out over the town and countryside with a different perspective and familiarity. I noticed a child by the castle door waving frantically at me. I waved back and he disappeared. Soon he returned with a group of children waving wildly and I could hear a faint chorus of "Jozee, Jozee." Little children, with their American hand-me-down clothes, had found me again.

Princess Ganga said, "The children knew you were coming and have been waiting for you." This only made things harder for me to tell them why I came. I was in such distress.

Princess Ganga and I walked to the school and met with George and the children. Even though they were out of school for the summer, they came together to put on a program for me. The children sang and danced.

"They have come such a long way in such a short time," I later said to Princess Ganga.

"I have never seen children learn as fast as these children," she informed me. "They learn this fast," as she snapped her fingers a few times.

"Isn't it amazing that these are the Untouchable children, the ones who are outcast, and supposedly not capable of learning," I said to her. "I hope the people in this community will notice that they are children too, no matter what caste they are from." Years would pass before I would hear the answer.

It was heartwarming to see what my seed money had started, but I was on another mission this time. Eventually I had to tell George, Princess Ganga, and Prince Bonnie that I could no longer be soliciting money for the school. I told them of the speeches I had made in New Delhi in the hopes of getting support for the school. I explained that I also had obligations to my own children. "You have to figure out a way to continue the school," I said. I saw the sadness on their faces. My heart broke. I had to do this. I felt that I had no choice. The money that I again brought and left behind would be enough to pay for the teachers for more than four years.

I spent a few days at the castle walking around, mingling with the community members and visiting with my friends, Princess Ganga and Prince Bonnie. Princess Ganga and I were driven back to Jaipur where I spent a few days at her home. I flew back to New Delhi, and from there I flew to Roma, Italy. I spent a week there and had not returned since my honeymoon. How ironic to be in Roma at a time that would have been my twenty-fifth wedding anniversary. This was a bizarre experience. How could I possibly have known that I would be returning, but this time alone?

Walking around Roma I started feeling the pleasures of life in the simple things. I felt that I had made a complete circle and had closed the door on my marriage. I knew I was living in the moment and not in the past. I wanted to savor this experience. I was surrounded by my fellow compatriots and speaking the language of my birth. It was as though I was having a rebirth of my own. I surrendered to the delight of being in this joy.

I sat on the Spanish Steps and shared wine with other tourists and my fellow Italians. I languished on the balcony of my hotel room one afternoon with a bottle of wine, a loaf of bread, some cheese, and olives. I loved the freedom that I was experiencing as I sat at a café on the corner of Barbarini Piazza. I was feeling life again. I explored Roma by jumping on various buses and allowing them to take me to wherever they were going. I sat on the benches waiting for the next bus and enjoyed the conversations with my fellow Italians. They treated me as one of their own, who had returned home. This was a new experience. To say that I found myself while in Roma seems like such a cliché, but I did. I felt whole for the first time in such a long time. I too was Italian!

I had my hair cut short, as I had seen on some of the Italian woman who passed by Trevi Fountain. I wanted a look that represented the new and liberated me. There seemed to be giddiness inside of me, as I kept saying repeatedly with a big smile, "I am alone . . . I am free . . . Isn't this great . . ." I declared and accepted my freedom. I was amazed to be experiencing this incredible bliss of happiness within me. The taste of freedom was a healing emotion.

I thought of the message I had left on William's phone, a few weeks earlier, and realized that I had my closure. I recalled that in one of our last conversations William had asked me to think of him while I was in Roma. I did, I mailed him a postcard with one sentence, "Having a wonderful time in Roma!"

The weight of the world was off my shoulders in many ways. This pit stop in my life seemed as though it was a reward for what I had gone through.

I flew to Sicily and spent a week with my sister Rosa in Carini. There again I visited Nonna and Nonno's grave. I recalled how the last time I had been there I had cried and had asked them to give me strength. I now came back and thanked them. I felt that somehow I had been nourished by their love, which it had reached and extended over onto me. It was only four short years since I had been there, but somehow it seemed like a lifetime.

"How incredible my life has changed in such a short time," I said to my sister Rosa. "Never in my wildest dreams could I have imagined the things I have done and experienced since I was here last." There was an acceptance to what life had waiting for me next

WHAT NOW

When I returned to America, I was ready, on so many levels. I accepted the fact that I would enter the graduate counseling program at SUNY Oneonta. I was opening up the mail I had left behind when I came across the acceptance letter from Albany University to enter their program for the Masters in Social Work, MSW. The letter had been there all along. I had not opened it before I left, thinking it was a soliciting letter from the university for my daughter. What was more amazing was that I had to reply by the day after I returned from Italy or the offer would be retracted.

The MSW program was what I had originally wanted. However, while in India, I had thought that the Albany MSW program was not available to me and that I should enter the counseling program at SUNY Oneonta. Now both doors were opened before me and I had to choose which door to go through. I thought about the decision overnight and decided that the timing was too coincidental. I was consciously aware of the serendipity of the circumstances, but I felt the true path that I should follow was to stay in Oneonta to pursue the counseling. The decision I had made in India, to go into the counseling program, I felt was based on Divine guidance. I chose to go through that door. I was seeing and feeling things differently. I was paying attention to what was being presented to me and the reasons for my choice.

When I returned from Italy and India there was another hearing with William for the disbursement of the house and finalization of the divorce. I had offered him a fair market value for the house. I could not give in to William's demands for more money. I stood firm on my offer for the sake of my children and our security.

William called me that evening. This time it was not in a friendly voice. He was so angry with me. I had forgotten the terror that he could instill within me. I was overwhelmed with his tone and negativity.

After hanging up, I burst into tears. I fell on my knees and forgave him for all the pain he had caused our family. The forgiveness came from within the depth of my being. I gave it freely, without reservations, stipulations, or conditions. I wished him well and released the last speck of him from my heart. This felt as though a weight had been lifted. I also realized that I no longer was responsible for keeping him sober. A vile growth seemed to have been removed from my body, as soon as I forgave him. Calmness and acceptance seemed to follow.

I will always be grateful to William for my wonderful children. In the last five years of our marriage, Louise and Albert had been turning against him. They were old enough to understand that their father had a drinking problem. The last year of our marriage had been the worst; both of the children had made negative remarks about his drinking, to his face.

The following morning William called. In a calm voice he informed me that he was ready to settle, sign the divorce papers, and turn the house over to me. It's rather amazing how this incident played out. Once I had forgiven him, he released the marriage and set me free. There seemed to be an understanding within me that forgiveness was the only thing I could control in life.

A few days before Christmas, Professor Ashok notified me that the school in Dundlod had closed. The people in the village convinced the old woman who had donated the cinder block room, to close the school. Professor Ashok said, "The village people do not believe these children should receive any special treatment, because they are from the Untouchable caste."

God, I said to myself, you could not have sent me half way around the world for nothing. I was devastated. This has to be part of your plan, right? If the school is closing then everything I experienced and went through was not real and was for nothing.

I walked around confused, unwilling to accept the fact that the school would close forever. I kept going over and over my mystical and spiritual experiences. I knew they were true but how could I justify them if the school closed. I struggled back and forth with this dilemma. I was pushed beyond the limitations of maintaining my belief and conviction. I was in such pain.

A few weeks later, we received word that Prince Bonnie had offered the children his horse stable within the castle walls for the continuation of the school. The children and the teachers cleaned out the horse stable. The school was now in the courtyard of the castle. This was another connection to my previous dream reality that this school was meant to be.

The castle was a tourist attraction for Prince Bonne's horse safari. Groups of people from Europe and the United States went there on retreat. The school within the castle walls was receiving attention. People started leaving small donations for the school and clothing for the children.

It would not have received any attention if it had stayed in the desert at the outskirts of the town. God's plans are certainly far greater than mine, I thought. Why did I ever doubt that God had His reasons for the closing of the original school? I was amazed at how things had worked out for the best. I thought about the universal wisdom of an Old Italian saying, said in various versions, "When God closes one door; He opens up a bigger door." He literally did just that—the castle door.

NO YOU CAN'T ASK THAT OF ME

The following spring, Professor Ashok was giving a speech on the Indo-International School in one of the college lecture halls. He introduced me and informed the audience how I had raised the money to start the school.

Three students approached me after the lecture. One student, a female, looked intently at me and asked, "What was your reasoning for raising the money and starting the school?"

"It is rather personal. I don't tell my story to just anyone."

She persisted with such authority and firmness, "You have to tell me! Please . . . ."

I reluctantly told her a small version of my spiritual experiences. When I finished she said, "You have no idea how I needed to hear this. Thank you." The other two students had not said a word during this time and just listened with interest.

I stood there stunned at her words and frozen to the spot, as they turned, walked away, and disappeared in the crowd. I wanted to stop them and ask her what she meant but I could not move. Her words sank into my soul. My hair stood on end. I felt a cold chill go through my body. My face must have drained of all color. I was in shock at the realization of what I internally understood. *I will have to write my spiritual and mystical experiences to share them with other people. I don't have the right to pick and choose who should hear of this extraordinary path I have walked. The book will find its way to people who need to hear of my journey and perhaps help them in their search for Truth.*

My reaction to this knowledge was swift and to the point,

"No! God, you can't possibly expect that of me. I went half way around the world for you and now you ask this of me? I cannot do that. I can't go out on a limb with this. Who would believe me? How can I possibly write a book? I do not know how to write a book. Someone else must have a book to write about this sort of stuff better than me. Go to someone else, please."

These were familiar words and I recalled the last time I had uttered them. I refused to further acknowledge the thought of the book. I shoved the thought to the back of my mind, but it was always there, nagging at me. Occasionally the dreaded thought would pop in my head, "I have to write the book." I would quickly answer back, "No, I don't." I felt as though there were two sides of me speaking to each other with such authority, strength, and conviction.

When the title of the book popped in my head, A Gift of My Own, I understood that eventually I would give in. I could fight this all I wanted, I could put it off as long as I could, but the time would come when I somehow would write the book.

LOVE IN ACTION

In the spring of 1999, I completed my master's program in counseling. I applied at many schools but could not obtain a counseling job for the fall. Once the window of opportunity was missed, I would have to wait another year. In January 2000, I decided to visit Mama and Papa, who were now living part-time in Naples, Florida. I might as well look in Florida and see if perhaps I might want to move there, I thought.

I also decided that the children in India needed a permanent building for the school. On my way down to Florida, I decided to make a stop in Washington D.C. I solicited Congressman Sherwood Boehlert to make arrangements for me to meet with Ambassador Naresh Chandra of India. My determination for the children and the school had given me the courage to do this.

I explained to Ambassador Chandra about the school, its location, and the importance of its continuation. I of course informed him of Prince Bonnie and Princess Ganga and how generous and supportive they had been with the school. He listened intently to what I had to say concerning the plight of the school. He then turned to his staff, men who were in the room, and asked them if they knew of the royal family. Some of his staff stated that they knew Prince Bonnie and his father. Prince Bonnie and King Rex were very much involved in politics in India.

When I had gone back to India, the second time, I had attended a birthday party with the royal family at a Parliament member's home in Jaipur. A man who was running for Prime Minister, and was from the Untouchable caste, was expected to attend. It was big news in India, and in most parts of the world, that such an event was taking place. At the last minute, unexpected circumstances prevented him from attending.

Most everyone spoke English at the party. They sat around exchanging pleasantries and discussing politics. The fact that a member from the Untouchable caste was running for Prime Minister was the topic of conversation. They all seemed to approve and were in favor of this opportunity. Dinner was buffet style, served late in the evening. Their custom is to serve dinner last and then the guests are expected to leave. It was an interesting evening and an opportunity to see the lifestyle of the upper class in India.

Ambassador Chandra asked one of his aids to look into the school. He assured me that he would do what was possible to support the school. Ambassador Chandra presented to me a book, Masterpieces of Indian Painting, published by Alice N. Heramaneck. As I was being escorted out of the building, my escort said, "You know, the Ambassador does not give this book to everyone."

"There, I have done all I can for the school. I cannot think of anything else to ensure the progress," I said to myself as I walked out of the Ambassador's office.

While in Florida Professor Ashok phoned me and said, "Jozie, I have good news. A couple from Elmira was staying at the castle and saw the plight of the children. They want to make a sizeable contribution to the school. The school is doing great and things are really looking up."

This was an emotional moment and I got choked up at hearing this news. "I will be back in March. Can you set up a meeting with this couple?" I asked. Professor Ashok agreed to set up a meeting for us. The couple resided over two hours away from where we live in Oneonta.

Professors Suzanne, Ashok, and I were excited to meet these people. I prepared lunch for all of us in my home. The couple donated one thousand dollars a year for life and an endowment would be set up to continue this donation. It was an exciting moment for all of us. This gave me hope. Some of the pressure was taken off of my shoulders. SUNY Oneonta and Professor Ashok got more involved with the school. This was a turning point for them to support and promote its continuation.

That spring I accepted a tutoring job working with migrant children in various schools in our area. I did not know it at the time, but this too would be in preparation for what was to come. Part of the job requirement was to visit the children's homes. In a country that is as bountiful as America, I did not expect to see such poverty.

This poverty was just as hard to accept as it had been in the streets of New Delhi. The poverty in the United States is hidden; it is beyond the railroad track, along a side street, or in tenement houses. It is in the trailer parks or in the woods off a dead end road. It was painful to see poverty again. I thought I had left it all behind me in India.

Yet, as poor as they were, they would still be considered middle class in India. I recalled mother Theresa's words, "The children of India are the poorest of the poor." As hard as it was, I was able to console myself and accept the poverty here. Not that anyone should ever accept poverty anywhere, on any level.

In the fall of 2000, I had not been able to obtain a job as a counselor. I could not understand that. Professor Suzanne suggested that I apply for a teaching position at the Oneonta Job Corps Academy. I had never thought of myself as a teacher. I was a counselor with a teaching certificate. I immediately got accepted.

I soon realized that I was teaching children with many disadvantages and in many ways they were America's Untouchable children. The students ranged in age from sixteen to twenty-four and most were African American or Hispanic. The students came from broken homes with unemployed adults and drug infested neighborhoods controlled by gangs. I was becoming aware of how God was working through me again.

I was no longer worried about the school in India because donations were pouring in from all over the world. The following year a French man, Mr. Franky Mulliez, out on his daily walk at the castle asked Princess Ganga, "What is going on in the horse stables?"

"It is a school for the Untouchable children," Princess Ganga stated. "I am hoping to collect $25,000 in order to build them a permanent school. We are constantly turning children away because we cannot accommodate them."

When Mr. Mulliez returned to Paris, he sent her a check for $25,000 to build the school, plus a yearly contribution. As you can imagine, nothing was surprising me any longer. Prince Bonnie donated a piece of land where the school would be built.

In May 2003, Princess Ganga and Prince Bonnie came to the United States. Princess Ganga was awarded an honorary doctorate degree from SUNY Oneonta. Professor Ashok has since received many accolades for his support with the school.

In 2004, Mr. Mulliez and Amber Trust of France sent funding for a vocational school to be built in conjunction with the Indo-International School. In 2005 the first students graduated from the vocational school and received certificates in English, Television, Radio Repair, Nursing Assistant, Computer Technician, Tailoring, Electronics, and Computer Application. The effect of this gift has rippled with love beyond the remote village. This light continues to shine because this is love in action.

LET GO AND LET GOD

Over the years I had the desire to return to Dundlod to see the final product of what the seed money had accomplished. There was one dream that I wanted to fulfill—to hand out the diplomas to the children at the Indo-International School. During the first part of July, 2005, that desire was fulfilled.

I flew to New Delhi airport. There was a lot of new construction going on around the airport. I stayed overnight in New Delhi and flew to Jaipur the following morning. Queen Jean picked me up at the airport with her chauffeur. It was nice to see my old friend. "Ganga," she explained, "is away for a few days."

I had been aware of that. Princess Ganga had planned her trip months before I had decided to come to India. Neither the Princess nor I could change our travel dates.

As we were driving on the way to the hotel in Jaipur, I could see that most of the buildings and fences were of a pale pink color. I asked Queen Jean, "How is it that everything appears to be pink?"

Queen Jean explained, "In 1853 the Prince of Wales, Edward Albert, son of Queen Victoria from England, visited Jaipur. In his honor, the whole city was painted pink to give it a mystical feel, to welcome him. This was during the regime of Sawai Ram Singh. The color became a tradition and people continue to paint their home in the same pink hue."

"So therefore it is called the Pink City. That was very interesting," I said. "For some reason I thought that there must have been a religious reason. I never thought it had a simple explanation." Queen Jean laughed.

I spent the next few days exploring and wandering around the temples and palaces of the Pink City. A few days later Princess Ganga came to pick me up. She jumped out of the taxi and we ran towards one another for a big hug. The last time I had seen the Princess was when she had been at SUNY Oneonta, two years earlier, to receive her honorary doctoral degree.

We had time to discuss many things on the three-hour trip to Dundlod. Princess Ganga explained that she had been on a retreat with her guru, Sai Baba, a famous spiritual leader in India. She gave me a book of his teachings.

Princess Ganga also informed me that she and Prince Bonnie had separated. She went on to explain, "There is a gulf between us and we are traveling on separate paths." I was heartbroken to hear this of my friends. To write the details would not be fair to either one of them.

It had been eight years since I had been to Dundlod. That was the time when I came to inform Princess Ganga, Prince Bonnie, and George that I no longer could continue soliciting money for the school. Shirag was six months old at the time.

As we turned into the main road of the castle, I could see that it was under construction. "Wow," I said, "this is great, they are fixing the road."

"There are many new things that are going on," Princess Ganga said. She pointed out the new school, high up on the hillside. Princess Ganga explained, "That road leads to the school. Bonnie had the road constructed in order to reach the land where the school is located. This has also opened up land for others to build new homes. George has a piece of land allocated to him to build a home next to the school. He will be able to move out of his apartment soon."

I had lunch with the royal couple and Sunina. Prince Bonnie proudly informed me of the progress of the school and the community. Prince Bonnie explained, "The school and the vocational center have uplifted the poorest of the poor to be self-sufficient in the area." He laughed with amazement. "Some of the graduates have opened up their own shops in the area while others have had the confidence to go into the cities looking for opportunities. Young women have been able to find work, support their families, and encourage their children of the benefit to having an education."

I was amazed, I said, "Really!"

"This school has transformed the community, the families, and the future of generations to come, as education continues to spread knowledge of the promise it brings to break the cycle of poverty," stated Prince Bonnie. "More families have moved to the area and new businesses have sprung up. The castle hotel is accommodating more people year around."

"Most important though," said Princess Ganga, "The Untouchable children are now accepted in the community. Many children from various caste systems are being bussed in. They all want to come to this school."

The truth that all children were accepted in the community was overwhelming and was a confirmation of what I had hoped to hear.

Prince Bonne's next statement was amazing, "The government has chosen Dundlod as one of two communities in India to use as a model to fix the water system, electricity, health services, education, restore temples, palaces, and roads. Did you see that the road coming into Dundlod was under construction?"

"Yes, I did see that," I said in amazement.

"That's part of the government's project," he explained.

Could it be that the seed I had planted with the group from Parliament, business people, and women, eight years earlier had taken root, I wondered? Now, after all these years, am I hearing the fulfillment of the, 'One Village at a Time' speech I had given in New Delhi? I recalled what Chandrika had said to me that day.

"Relax Jozee, you have planted a good seed. They have heard you. It takes time for the Indian people to do something."

I was stunned at what I was hearing, an affirmation of the speech I had given. I understood the reasons I had to return—to hear all the accomplishments that had been achieved. "Okay that's it. What more proof could I possibly want to know that the hand of God was in this community?"

George came by in the afternoon. It was good to see my old friend. I inquired about Shirag. He took me to see him.

Shirag was now nine years old and attending the school. It was wonderful to see how he had grown. He was tall for a boy his age, with shiny black hair and bright dark eyes. He wore shorts and a white shirt and was barefoot of course. George explained that his parents were in the city looking for work.

Shirag bent down and kissed my feet, a tradition that shows respect. George translated. Shirag said, "I know you; you are my Auntie from America."

George explained that he knew of me and how I had been present when he was born.

I said, "I know what your name means, a light that shines in the dark."

He smiled and asked, "Why have you not come sooner, Auntie?"

"It's not that easy. I wish I could have. I have never forgotten you or the children in this community," I said. I gave Shirag a jacket. He was very pleased that it was from America. He gave me a big hug when I left.

George and I walked over to the cinder block room that had been the original school. I was overcome with thoughts of how that room had paved the way for all the changes in this community. We walked by the new school and saw the transformation of how the gift had grown. I was not ready to go into the new school. I needed time to regroup my feelings because of all the emotions that I was experiencing.

George said that the children and their parents would be at the school the following morning. He went on to explain that there was no school in summer but the children and their parents would be there anyway, wanting to welcome me. I thought that would be a great time to take an overview of the new school.

The following morning George was prompt and walked Princess Ganga and I to the school. Princess Ganga spoke to the children and their parents in the Hindi language. Even though I could not understand, I was able to pick out words such as pizza. I realized she was informing them of how the money had been raised to start their school. They periodically would burst out clapping. Princess Ganga had to tell them to stop and wait until she was done. When she was finished, they all stood up and clapped enthusiastically. I spoke next and Princess Ganga translated for me. I know that I told them I was thrilled to be there but the rest is fuzzy. I was overcome with emotion.

I have often wondered what they would have thought if I had informed them of my spiritual journey that had led me to their community. Perhaps someday I could stand before them to reveal the inner revelation and gift that had been entrusted to me for their community. The truth is that it was God's gift, not mine.

That day I was able to touch and see the nine years of growth since I had first arrived to this humble community. Look what God has done, I thought. Why had it been so difficult to let go and let God?

The success of the school was my confirmation that my spiritual experiences had really happened. I should have known that it would not fail, as I had heard the answer in the church, four months before I left for India. "You cannot fail, its God's plan, not yours." How little faith I had.

I was able to touch the children that day. I had thought of them often over the years and here I was hugging them. The girls were beautiful in their sky blue salwar-kameez, which is a two-piece outfit seen often in New Delhi. The salwar resembles a pajama and tapers at the ankles. The kameez, which resembles a long shirt, is worn over the salwar. A long white silk scarf is draped loosely around their necks, flowing in the back. The boys wore dark blue pants and white shirts. Ganga had chosen the uniforms for the children, which were paid for by contributions to the school.

The children presented a wonderful program for me. They danced, sang, and read poetry. Afterwards I handed-out certificates to all the children. I gave each of them gifts such as pencils, pens, crayons, coloring books, sunglasses, and calculators. When I ran out of those supplies, I handed out an assortment of candies.

The family members were nicely dressed, anxious to shake my hand and smile at me. It was such a joy to be with them. They had such bright smiles and were so happy to have gotten the small gifts. They were grateful that their children had been given this wonderful educational opportunity. The children were very proud of the English they had learned and spoke to me with the few words they knew.

George, who was one of the first teachers hired, was now the principal. He is dedicated to the belief and the promise that education brings. He showed me around the large and spacious building with the courtyard in the middle. There was a library but only a few shelves were filled with books. George explained that they now had six teachers at the school. In the evenings, classes are held for women to learn to read and write, so they could correspond with their children who may live far away. A food bank had been started in the school for the needy. Lunches were being served to the children. A company in Sweden had given numerous computers to the school; the children were now connected to the world.

George brought me to the flat rooftop of the school. He explained that it had been built in a way that it would accommodate a high school on the second floor at a future time. There was a breathtaking view of the town below on one side and the desert on the other. I watched as two men rode camels on the desert side. I waved at them and they waved at me. "Only in India," I said to George, "could I wave at men going by on camels while standing on the roof of a school in view of a castle."

Princess Ganga and I walked back to the castle. I was quiet and subdued at the many affirmations of my spiritual experiences. Princess Ganga said statements that stopped me in my tracks. "Of all the people in the world, God picked you to start this school. You are the mother of this school, you brought the seed money."

Those statements humbled me. "I do not know why He picked me," I said. "I am overwhelmed at the magnitude of your words."

I was moved by what had been accomplished since 1996. The school has become a beacon of light, showing what can be accomplished when people put their energy and love towards helping others. This school and the community have become a model for others to follow.

In 2006, Mr. Mulliez donated an additional $25,000 to build a high school on the rooftop. I have never met Mr. Mulliez and I am sure he does not know of me, but we are connected in the most incredible and unusual way. It would be a dream to meet him someday. As I am writing these words, the high school is being dedicated and is ready to open. How ironic that this book is being written, as the final chapter of the school is being completed.

The existence of the school has spread via the tourist groups which stay at the castle. College students from the United States and Europe come to the school to do their internships and work with the children. The school has touched people all over the world.

As I was departing India I thought of the definite affirmations that God's hand was in this remote village of Dundlod. God's hand had connected people from all over the world to become part of this light that shines in the dark. But I also knew that I was no more responsible for the school than I was for the poverty of India. If anything, it was accomplished in spite of me. The school and all the changes that have followed are examples of God's love, by bringing people together to achieve a miracle. I am nothing more than an instrument in His planning and I must have been one of His toughest cases.

I could not help but wonder if I would ever again have the opportunity to return to Dundlod and visit the school and the wonderful people I befriended there.

After leaving India I flew to Italy, where I met my daughter Louise. We spent a week in Roma. Louise had just completed her Master's degree in Science from the University at Binghamton. I was very excited to have this opportunity to show one of my children, Louise, our roots. She had always pointed out that she was "American" whenever I had called her "Italian".

Louise had arrived in Roma a few days before me and was exuberant when we caught up. She was in love with Italy. She was suddenly Italian. It was thrilling to see the connection she had discovered to our roots. We did the usual tourist things like the Colosseum, Trevi Fountain, the Spanish Steps and of course Saint Peter's Cathedral. She went on to visit her cousins in Milan and I flew back home to the United States.

The following year Louise returned to Italy to attend her cousin Valeria's wedding in Carini. She then backpacked the rugged portion of the coast on the Italian Riviera, in the Liguria region of Italy. Louise explored and fell in love with Cinque Terre. I now have to remind her that she is *American,* as well as the first generation of an Italian immigrant. It's wonderful to see her proud of her Italian heritage.

Perhaps one of the most endearing thoughts Louise said to me while we were together in Roma was, "Mom I am proud of you. You believed that you had to go to India and you did. I now understand why you made that decision. Maybe someday I can go back with you."

"There was never any doubt in my soul that I had to go to India, but there was doubt in my mind," I said. "To go to India with you would be wonderful. Perhaps together we can do something for that small fishing village in Mahabalipuram." Louise had given me the most resistence when I had gone to India. I was glad to see that my daughter had grown and accepted my journey.

Waiting my turn to speak to the Parliament men
& women, and business people in New Delhi.

Queen Jean, me, & King Rex at a birthday party.

Speaking at a Business Women's luncheon in New Delhi.

Visiting Gandhi's shrine in New Delhi.

Visiting with Shirag.

Bringing clothes & school supplies to the children at the
Indo-International School. George & the children look on.

In Italy, at the Trevi Fountain, with a new haircut.

Section 4

IN THE ATTITUDE OF SILENCE, THE SOUL
FINDS THE PATH IN A CLEARER LIGHT, AND
WHAT IS ELUSIVE AND DECEPTIVE RESOLVES
ITSELF INTO CRYSTAL CLEARNESS.

OUR LIFE IS A LONG AND ARDUOUS
QUEST AFTER TRUTH.

Mahatma Gandhi

TRANSFORMATION

I was discussing this book with my sister-in-law, Marianne. She was recuperating from a shoulder operation and inquired about the book I was writing. I asked if she would like me to read it to her. She came to America as a young bride from Carini, Italy and had difficulty reading English. For a few days, I went to her home, kept her company, and read it aloud. This was the first time I had read the entire manuscript from beginning to end.

I read statements I did not know I had written, and frequently came away saying, "Oh my God. I can't believe I wrote this." It was the first time that I saw the relationship and connections to the experiences, laid out before me. I was amazed by the synchronism and correlation of the spiritual events. For the first time I understood how the chaotic trials in my life had to occur in sequence, for the path to be cleared, in preparation for a higher purpose, bigger than myself. I was amazed to see the particulars; the cohesiveness and simplicity of how each event had unfolded, in relation to how each had been built on the other. It was startling to discover my whole life, laid out in a beautiful tapestry.

I now understood how the humanism in me had been a reluctant participant in this reality. Subconsciously, I was aware that there was a higher purpose for my experiences. The ego, the humanism, had to step aside before flowing into the realm of spirituality. I had been a reluctant child during spiritual moments.

I was humbled when I realized how little faith and trust I had in the Divine. I saw for the first time how I needed the school to succeed in order to confirm my spiritual experiences. How strong my faith should have been; and yet, I am human with human vulnerabilities. I could not surrender the doubts, and at the same time, I believed. This is the vulnerability of being human, which is a gift from God, the freedom to make choices.

During the spiritual encounters, there was complete abandonment, no fear, or doubt, but pure conviction of the reality of the moment. The magical feeling of bliss would quench the struggles and the doubts during those periods.

I could not make up these experiences, without having lived them. I fought writing them down for ten years; yet, when it was time to write them, it was as though I was experiencing them all over again. This was the only way that the authenticities of those moments could be written.

Marianne then asked me two questions that made me stop and think. "How have you changed? What have you learned?"

Amazingly, I had never thought of these questions before. A mirror was now placed before me and I was forced to look within in order to formulate the answers.

God has changed me in many ways. I am grateful that I am not one of those 'holier than thou people.' I did not want to live up to what I believe to be a false perception, which is an individual who will place himself above others who do not believe as he does. A person who has experienced Truth will be enlightened in the acceptance of other's journeys. Everyone's journey is his or her own, and is dictated by his or her beliefs. My journey is mine and everyone has to discover his own. To impose my beliefs on others is to lose my authentic self. I do not have the right to judge others' journeys. The journey of being human is to strive towards self-actualization, which leads to liberation, the gift of being. These are universal Truths.

The ego is part of being human and does not exist in the spiritual realm, which will be discarded at death, with the human body. One's self-image is an aspect of being human. The entrance to spirituality is experienced within, where Truth exists.

The structures of this world, such as language, do not apply in mysticism. Thought forms, transpired during spiritual moments, are revealed by inner revelation. They are expressed in fundamental ways and correlate to the individual's understanding.

There is a self-awareness of my connection to humanity and to the spirit of others. I accept the differences and see beauty in the uniqueness of the individual, regardless of sexual orientation or religious affiliation. I am aware of the light within my path; and therefore, make room for others to walk their journey. There is attentiveness towards strangers, in what I say to them and in what I hear from them.

Evilness, the devil, hell, are deep-rooted fears created by the primal minds of man. It is a human concept to believe that if there is good, there must be bad. Evilness is a void, which exists in the psyche of humanity, fanned by manmade doctrine and superstition. Where there is Love, evil cannot exist. The only evilness is that which is created in the hearts of man. These battles are being fought in the mind.

The storm within me has passed. I see and feel things differently. I have learned that life is a continuous challenge through many journeys. When one journey ends, another begins. I have been able to accept the obstacles in life with the mantra that repeats in my soul, "*This too shall pass.*" I am aware of the beauty and wonders of life and the simplicity of humankind. I have been humbled in every sense of the word.

The joys are deeper and the intensity of pain is less. I pay attention to my thoughts and understand the strength they have when they are released in the universe. I pay attention to the subtle nudges in life and the direction they are taking me. I have learned that the replay of yesterday or the worry for tomorrow will not add one precious second to the failure or success of those intangible moments.

The gift of life is that I am a spiritual being, having a human experience. The thought of expecting more of me, because of my spiritual experiences, is a reminder of my humanity. I am still just a being of this world. At the beginning of my journey I had asked not to be changed. This request was a thought form that I would not lose my authentic self.

The times that I wonder and question my experiences quickly pass. I know that they really happened. A gift that I have been given is to have experienced these amazing spiritual events. The wonder of the numinous occurrences is too elusive to put into words. An individual who has experienced the magical feeling of bliss can identify with the reality of my perceptions.

I now see changes in my life as opportunities to grow and I wonder where they will take me. I do descend into a well of darkness at times of crisis, but the climb out is much easier. It is as though the battles that go on in the mind, eventually, become moments of clarity, despite the knowledge of vulnerability and being human.

The struggles of life are similar to the story of the boy who tried to help a butterfly out of its cocoon by cutting the casing. The butterfly withered and died without the physical struggle of having strengthened its wings. The struggles in my life have made me stronger and taught me to fly. My transformation is that I had been in a cocoon and now am transformed into a butterfly.

THE JOURNEY

As the final section of this book is being written, I still marvel at the events in my life. The saying goes, 'Life happens when you are not looking.' I certainly have had one interesting life, but I was not aware of the journey while it was happening. Only when the journey unfolded was I able to see my life in astonishment and incredulity.

Understanding how God has worked through me to accomplish what He wanted is rather amusing and beyond amazement. I have questioned many times over the years, "Why me Lord? I am nobody." I did not expect an answer.

Out for a walk one day, I again started to ask the proverbial question. Before I had finished I heard the familiar gentle soft voice, filled with love and compassion. I heard the words in my left ear, entering my soul, "You are one of the chosen ones."

I have stopped questioning and have accepted what I believe to be, that on my soul level, I consented to this path, this journey.

Perhaps the reason is simple. The little girl inside of me is forever present. I have never lost the child-like qualities and I am still amazed at the wonders of life. People over analyze the unexplainable and search for human logic. To accept human explanations is to become lost in logic, because there is no logic in spirituality, only an inner knowing. Searching for Truth is within, which is available to all those who knock and seek; they will find.

Writing this book is part of my journey, which would not be complete until the words have been written. Knowing that I would have to give in, to the increasingly nagging thoughts that I must write the book, was no easy task. I knew the time had come for me to write the book and I could not put it off any longer. The thought was now constantly up front and I could not push it back. I kept putting it off by finding excuses and saying, "I don't know how to write a book. Where do I begin? What if this book were published? Would the reader not believe me, or worse, put me on a pedestal?"

The most significant reason for not wanting to write this book was the fear that I could lose the essence of the wonderment. Would I continue to receive those internal jolts of joy and understanding? Could I become no different from the person whose motivation is to receive accolades or to be written about in the newspaper? As usual, I placed obstacles before me because I was also afraid of wandering into the unknown.

The desk, where the computer sat, was in a confined area in the spare bedroom. I wanted to move the furniture around in the room before I began to write the book. I knew that this was an excuse I was using. Over the years I had meant to ask someone to help me change the room around, but would forget, and remember only after they had left. This excuse served me well, putting off what I knew I eventually would have to do.

One day my son Albert came home and I finally remembered to ask him to help me move the desk. "Albert, can you help me move this bedroom around so we can place the desk in the opposite side of the room? It is time I wrote about India and my spiritual experiences. It would be more comfortable to place the desk on the other side of the room."

I had removed the barrier; I had voiced the commitment, and there was no turning back. I was stunned. I acknowledged what I had to do and I knew the time had come to write the book. I felt as though the voice within was telling the voice in my head what I had to do. For a week I would walk by the bedroom, stand at the doorway, look at the computer, and ask myself, "Why should I put myself in such a vulnerable position to write this book?"

Many times over the years, I would go to a bookstore and browse, waiting for a book to find me. It seemed as though the book I needed would fall off the shelf while I was reaching for another, or would stick out of the bookshelf, or a friend would give it to me. It always seemed to be the perfect book for me to read at that time, to give me comfort, clarification, or affirmation.

To write this book was no exception. "Okay", I said. "If the time has come, then I will have some kind of affirmation and acknowledgment." I went to the bookstore in search of the perfect book to give me ideas on how to get started.

I was standing in the aisle looking through the bookshelves when I heard a thump next to me, the noise of a book hitting the floor. A woman retrieved it. I looked at her and said, "You know, whenever I drop a book, it always seems to be the perfect book I need to read." I watched her as she looked at the title, smiled, and placed the book back on the shelf. I continued my search on the bookshelves. A thought nagged me, which would not go away. Finally, turning to her, I said, "Okay, maybe that book is meant for me. Which book was it?"

She searched in the bookshelves, retrieved the book, and handed it to me. I smiled at the knowledge that was being presented before me. My heart leapt with a knowing. The words on the cover, 'Spiritual Writing', popped out at me. I received the confirmation to my question; and yet, more affirmation was to come.

Feeling that I owed the woman an explanation I said, "I have been thinking of writing my memoirs of my spiritual journey and came here in search for an answer".

To my amazement she replied with such authority and conviction, "Well you got your answer. You *should* write about your spiritual journey."

She had reaffirmed and acknowledged what I had been

stalling to do. As usual, I had to be pushed to complete this part of the journey. It was later that I thought, "Could she have been an angel to remind me that the gift I had been given was yet to fully unfold?"

That night I read the introduction of the book, 'The Best American Spiritual Writing 2005, edited by Philip Zaleski and published by Houghton Mifflin Company. I closed the book and said, "It's time." I did not need any more confirmation for what I had to do; and yet, I had no idea of how or where I was to begin.

In the middle of the night I was suddenly awakened. It was three thirty-three in the morning and I immediately went to the computer. I sat before it, perplexed by what I was doing awake at that hour. I was staring at a blank page on the computer, my fingers poised, not knowing where or how to begin. I also realized that for years previously I had been periodically awakened at three thirty-three in the morning. I would look at the clock, turn over, and go back to sleep. It did not matter if the clocks had changed, if I were in another country or on another continent. I would awaken at that hour and wonder, "What significance does this time have for me?" This had always intrigued me. I now understood the meaning. This was another acknowledgment that the time had come for me to write the book.

So there I sat intently looking at the empty computer screen and said loudly, "You want this book written Lord? Well you are going to have to help me because I don't know what to do or where to begin."

This book then came to life, without ever struggling for what needed to be written. I never planned how or what I was going to write. The titles of the chapters were written before I even knew what I was going to write about. I was consumed, never rereading what I had written, and not knowing where I was going with it. It was unfolding on its own.

It seemed as though I had stepped aside and my soul was revealing what needed to be written. For three weeks, I wrote feverishly. I surrendered to the mystery that was unfolding before me. I have been amazed with this wonder. The realization that I had started writing this book, on the first weekend in September, exactly ten years from when I had left for India with my fellow travelers, is rather amusing. If there is one thing this reluctant traveler has learned, it is that it always has been God's timing, not mine. This too was no coincidence.

I was drained after three weeks of writing the book. I could not go near the manuscript for a year, until the following September, of 2007, when I knew the opportunity had come before me again, to do what I had to do—finish the book. Writing this book has released the final gift that was given to me. This gift is for everyone who reads it.

THE CALLING TO THE GIFT

My friend Maureen and I were discussing books we had recently read. Since she had read my manuscript she asked me, "Tell me about the book you read, The Best American Spiritual Writing 2005."

"I never read the book, only the introduction."

She looked at me in shock, "You never read the book? How could you not have read the book?"

"I did not want to be influenced by what was written, so I never read it."

"You have to read it, now! There may be a message in there that is meant just for you."

I was amazed at her persistence. That night I snuggled up in bed and opened to the first story in The Best American Spiritual Writing 2005. I bolted up in bed as I read the title, 'The Gift of the Call,' by Christopher Bamford from the Parabola magazine. I was amazed! I had been struggling with the title for my book, 'A Gift of My Own' and wondering whether it was a good title. This was an affirmation that I had the right title. This was another synchronism at this time in my life.

What is rather amusing is the fact that as a young girl it appeared to me that everyone around me had a special gift or talent to call his or her own. My friends could draw, paint, write, ride horses, or play an instrument. As a young woman, I noticed my sister Rosa could sew, paint, and crochet; I would have settled for one of them. My brothers, Antonio, Francisco, and Giuseppe, are very successful business people in whatever they do.

Everyone seemed to have something special or a gift to call his or her own. There was a feeling inside of me always, that I had no special gift or talent. There was a feeling of searching and waiting for my special gift or talent to come. Amazingly, I would inwardly say, teasingly and wistfully, "God, you gave everyone a special gift but me . . . . Where is my gift? Did you forget me?"

I certainly had never expected an answer! In time, His time, He answered me. He called me to give me my gift and what did I say? "No, go to someone else please". God must have a sense of humor, especially when calling me. I do not know what He was thinking when He entrusted me with the greatest gift of all—to bring the gift of love and light to a remote village in the desert, an opportunity to feed God's poorest of the poor.

THE GIFT THAT KEEPS ON GIVING

Indo-International School is a small contribution for humankind. The effect that the school has had on the Dundlod community has rippled to touch people around the world. This could only be God's work. The light that shines from the seed that the Divine wanted to plant was, Love in Action, the Indo-International School. This gift of love extends, embraces, and grows.

This has been a gift, which keeps on giving.

As I am completing this aspect of the book, Princess Ganga informed me that the Indo-International School continues to grow in the momentum of love. I am reminded of what Mother Teresa said; "I could not have picked up the other thousand children if I had not picked up the first."

There is a quote I once heard a commentator state, that Jacqueline Kennedy Onassis had said, which has stayed with me. "If you bungle raising your children, I don't think whatever else you do matters very much."

My son Albert and his wife Bridget are happily married and presented me with a beautiful granddaughter, Ayla Louise on July 28, 2008. They own a successful restaurant called *Mama Giuseppa* in Endicott, New York.

My daughter Louise has just completed her PhD from the University of Michigan in Applied Physics and is working at Birmingham University, in Alabama. I am very close, as close as any loving mother could possibly be, to my wonderful adult and successful children. *They have been beacons of light and love in my life.*

Then there are the hundreds of children whom I have loved and touched at the Oneonta Job Corps Academy. They are the lives I have helped to redirect their return to society for the betterment of their future, to become productive citizens. *They have been rays of hope within me.*

The other children in my life are the children of India. They are nursing assistants, computer operators, tailors, and small appliance repairers. They own small businesses and have improved their lives and the futures of thousands and thousands of children that are yet to be. They are able to go out into the world to contribute to society and their families for generations to come, as they spread the success of education. *They have nourished my soul immensely.*

If I measured myself by the success of children whom I have touched, then I have not bungled life. Nothing else really matters. I have gone beyond my own expectations.

I have started getting the familiar burst of love and joy inside of me lately. I know what this means. My life is about to change again. I have come to a fork in the path of my life. New players have entered while others have left my stage. I know that I am about to embark on yet another path less traveled. I already have said my standard statements to God. "No, absolutely not—I am done. I did everything you wanted me to do. I went half way around the world for you. I wrote this book, which has been nagging at me for ten years. Now you ask more of me? I cannot do it. Please go to someone else. Somebody has got to know what you are asking better than I do."

I refuse to think about it and have shoved it to the back of my mind.

I know that eventually I will give in, because there will be a hunger, thirst, and the burning desire to want more and I will follow.

Upon my return from India, family and friends would

periodically ask me the proverbial question, "Are you done with India now?"

There is only one answer to that question and that is to answer with another question, "Are God and India done with me?"

THE MYSTERIOUS STRANGER

I completed the manuscript—sat back—and said, "It is done."

I barely finished saying the words when a vision came into view from within. It was a familiar vision and one that included the mysterious stranger. I had experienced this vision when I was in the castle in Dundlod, India when I had been there with my fellow travelers. We had been in India almost three months, the school was completed, and I was out of money. Before falling asleep that evening, I questioned whether I had accomplished what I had been sent to do and why I was even in India. Both of these thoughts contradicted each other; and yet, that was the reality of my thinking at that moment. I was missing my children and my familiar life and at the same time, I wanted confirmation that my time in India had not been in vain. Looking back it seemed as though I had a lucid moment of the reality of being in India. The following is what I experienced in my dream reality that night.

I was bending down, bottle-feeding a baby lamb. Next to the lamb were feet in sandals, peeking out of a white robe. Instinctively I knew it was Jesus. Next to Jesus was another individual with bare feet poking out of a white tunic. A wooden staff was by his side. His identity was not internally revealed. Looking sideways next to me, I understood was my cousin Rosa holding a chubby baby girl in her arms, with her legs dangling, facing Jesus, and the man in the white tunic. I could not see any faces.

Following the dream reality occurrence, the doubts for being in India were alleviated, by the insightful knowledge that followed. The desire to analyze or speculate whom the identity of the unrevealed man had not been a problematic concern.

Over the years, I would recall the vision and see the feet but I still would not speculate on the identity of the man with the wooden staff. I would shove the vision aside and think, "I am not ready to know." I knew that the answer was there, when I was ready. What mystified me more than the identity of the man was the fact that I was not ready to acknowledge his identity. I understood that I would know when the time came for this inner knowledge to be revealed.

So here I sat, the book completed, with the vision of the bare feet with the wooden staff. I knew the time had come because I felt this inexplicable feeling that the consciousness of the barefoot man holding the wooden staff was ready to be known. "Ok," I said, "I am ready. Who are you?"

Before I had even finished saying the words, a familiar smiling toothless face came into view. I smiled back at him with the inner knowledge as to who he was. There was immediate clarification of knowledge flooding me, unraveling and revealing our connectedness. This wonder and mystery perplexed and stunned me.

I was humbled. I sat there bewildered and dazed as inner awareness bombarded my soul as each piece of my journey connected to this final mystery. Even with all the mysticism I had experienced along my journey, I was still astounded. I had an understanding that *he* had been my constant companion in India.

I recalled that I had picked up a book of his quotes the previous summer at my local bookstore. I had gone in with the intention of just browsing around, not an unusual procedure for me. Walking into a bookstore is exhilarating and I become lost in thought as I browse through the books. I rarely venture in with the intention of buying a book. I have numerous books at home waiting to be read.

Walking around the bookstore, I picked up a small book of quotes by Mahatma Gandhi. I was drawn to the book and found myself picking it up a third time. Not understanding, I felt, inexplicably, that this book had picked me. I bought it, not thinking much about it and shoved it in the bookshelves at home, with the intention of reading it at a future date.

Still stunned I retrieved the book from my bookshelves, The Words and Inspiration of Mahatma Gandhi, Peace—published in 2007 by Blue Mountain Press, introduction by Desmond Tutu. On the cover was that smiling familiar face I had just envisioned. I opened the book and there was a picture of Gandhi, barefoot, holding a wooden staff. I read these quotes, 'Truth resides in every human heart, and one has to search for it there and to be guided by truth as one sees it. But no one has a right to coerce others to act according to his own view of truth.' Those words summed up the reasons for my journey, as well as Gandhi's philosophy of life.

Throughout my journey, I had felt a connection to Gandhi but did not understand the reason for it other than our link to India. I now realized that it was much deeper and on a spiritual level. Gandhi's love from the other side had reached out and I had felt his consciousness. I had been a spectator and his companion on a journey that he wanted to complete. His essence had been with me. I had absorbed his inner knowledge and the love for his country and people. He took this journey through me, and I was experiencing this wonder. His energy and love had walked in my shoes. His love from the other side reached out and connected to help his fellow man.

I could not go near the manuscript for three months as I contemplated, acknowledged, and connected this inner revelation about my journey. I needed time to process and accept this internal consciousness. I was in awe.

The signposts had been there all along but I had not known how to read them. The mere fact of the unusual love and connection I had with the children and people of India should have given me the first clue. I understood now the reasons why I was not meant to know until the journey was complete. This knowledge would have been overwhelming at that time.

Gandhi's belief in nonviolence and his emancipation of the people of India from the British Empire is well documented. What I was amazed to read was what defined Gandhi—his empathy, compassion, and love for the Untouchable people, compatriots, and humankind. He personifies a true altruism; he gave his life for the greater good of others, for humanity.

He was intensely passionate, loved the children of India, and he held the belief that all men are created equal. I had seen that genuine smile in the woman making the cow patties in Varanasi. I had felt Gandhi's compassion for the children with leprosy. I saw the same smile and determination on the thin men on the bicycle contraptions that drove people around. I saw the indomitable spirit in all the Untouchable children, his children. It was with his thoughts and passion that I spoke in front of the parliament and various business people. It was his goal to help the poor. I had been his instrument.

I was amazed to read the many things that Gandhi believed in, that I had unknowingly learned myself, along my journey. He professed that all religions are one and that they all lead to the same source. He called the essence of God, Truth. He fought against the oppression of the Untouchable people and the caste system. He believed that education would pave the way for freedom, removing superstition, bondage of poverty, and the caste system. Gandhi believed that the rich should provide for the poor and give part of their land to them.

I do not compare myself to being anything like Gandhi; I was his vessel for the greater good of the people of India, his India. This was the last missing link for complete understanding of my journey, and I was not meant to know this, until I finished writing this entire book. Gandhi was able to put into perspective the reason for my journey. We were on a mission together to put love into action. I completed what he would have wanted to do.

MY FELLOW TRAVELERS

Over the years, I have thought of my fellow travelers often and periodically tried to locate them, more so when I was writing this book. I have been able to locate a few of them. I posed three questions to them: Why did you choose to go to India? What did you take from it? How did it change you?

MAGEN LEE SHAW

"I went to India because I knew this would probably be the only chance I would get to have such an experience. I was interested in their culture and religion. I wanted to be thrown right into the middle of it to learn more. I thought the program was so different from other study abroad programs because it incorporated six weeks of community service, which I was thrilled to be a part of.

Like you, I never quite realized how spoiled and sheltered we were in America until I saw firsthand how many people in other parts of the world live. It was an adjustment when we went to India and an equal adjustment coming home. The words, "enough", "normal", "clean", "luxury", "personal space", etc. all took on new meaning! I feel extremely lucky now, to have easy access to good medical care, some level of protection from diseases, and to have so many comforts and "luxuries" (it's amazing how the little things everyone takes for granted ARE actually LUXURIES). I know that I want to someday take my children traveling all over the world so they too can have that new perspective. It's so very important. Also, I will never forget the bonds we formed with each other throughout that experience. I will always love my fellow travelers as well. Now I am a mother of two and a registered nurse in neonatal intensive care. I love my job and I love making a difference in the lives of the babies and their families. I work in a state hospital, so I am confronted with many different cultures every day. My India experience probably gave me a better ability to be open minded, understanding, and sensitive to these differences. I still have my personal struggles in my life, but I try to stay on the path of growing and evolving. I will forever have the travel bug!"

JENNIFER BORST—
"I did a semester in India because I wanted to experience a third world country. I was into Eastern Indian philosophy (Hindu and Buddhist) as well as their poetry and imagery. I was taking an Eastern philosophy class at Fredonia at the time.

I came away with knowledge of the Hindi language and Eastern ways of life such as not using the left hand for anything but wiping yourself. I also have a lot of memories of temples and the iconography at the temples such as statues of Ganesh, Shiva, Krishna, and Kali. I have memories of the tropical and desert landscapes, peacocks, cows wandering the streets and eating garbage. I also recall the crazy and chaotic traffic that didn't always obey rules such as stop lights and stop signs. It seemed driving required a lot of negotiation with other drivers.

I have greater appreciation for my independence, respect for strangers, our food, clothing, transportation, roads, and essentially material goods that weren't always readily available there.

My status now is that I am married, have a full time job, but not quite at what I want to be doing. I am a Case Coordinator in a group home for adolescents with a mental health diagnosis. I am working towards developing some kind of art therapy either for myself, independent practice or with an established agency.

AMBER REHLING

"The SUNY Oneonta trip was actually my second trip to India. My first expedition to India was about two years before the SUNY trip. At that time I spent a few months in Tamil Nadu, doing volunteer work at a school. My motivation for that trip was purely my own sense of adventure, really nothing more complicated than that. I've met many people who went to India because it was a long-time dream, or because they were fascinated by the culture or traditions, but that was not my case! I knew very little about India, in fact, I just wanted to try my hand at teaching and to travel to some place new and exciting. I was overwhelmed at first and didn't know if I really liked it, but then it really grew on me. The more I saw and experienced, the more curious I became; and I also, have to say that the people really made an impression on me with their kindness. At the end of that first trip, I realized I had just scratched the surface of what there was to know about India and I wanted to go again and do more. The biggest thing I gained from that first trip was a greater openness to other people and to new experiences.

The SUNY Oneonta trip was the one that I chose to do partly as a way to go back to India; but also, because I thought the aspect of having classes while we were there and doing volunteer work would make it a richer experience, of which it definitely did. I gained immensely from the SUNY Oneonta trip! We had some very interesting classes about Indian history, culture, philosophy and religion. I still recall many of the things I learned.

Above all however, I had some very eye-opening experiences in our exchanges with local people. One experience that really made an impression on me was one time when we did volunteer work for Princess Ganga, a speech therapist who was doing hearing test for children in villages in Rajasthan. I heard about how complicated it was for children with hearing impairments to be able to get any basic services and help. This made a deep impression on me, because I was hearing impaired as a small child

240

myself, and there was no question at that time about me getting the medical attention I needed or doing speech therapy-that was a given. On the other hand, a child in India is not likely to get medical attention due to lack of resources.

I also witnessed what a tremendous difference the care and concern of a small number of people can make in the lives of others. I especially loved our experience doing volunteer work for the Spastics Society, which helps people with cerebral palsy. Josie and I spent a week at a small school that was an offshoot of the Spastics Society, and I was really moved by seeing the care and love that the teachers had for the children there. The children we worked with had severe disabilities, and were unable to talk due to their lack of muscle control. The teachers taught them to make simple sounds for "yes" and "no", and based on that simple ability, the teachers were able to engage them in genuine conversations.

Of course, the crowning moment of our volunteer work was the opening of the Indo-International School in Dundlod. The fact that our group was able to initiate a project like that with such modest resources still amazes me. The growth of the school is astonishing.

I haven't gone back to India (yet!) but I have had other international experiences. After I graduated from San Francisco State, I went to live in Normandy, France for about 5 years. I worked in the English department at a few high schools. Presently I live and work in San Francisco, where I have been alternating between teaching elementary school and teaching English as a second language for adult students.

I still think back often about my experiences in India, and very much hope to go back when the time is right."

PATRICK HICKEY

"It was a cold winter in Binghamton when I found out about the India program. I was searching for a place to warm up, and I couldn't think of a place hotter than India. It was exotic. It was romantic. It was steeped in mystic tradition. It seduced me with its promise of mystery and adventure. It had great food. And it was hot.

I'd been a traveler in the States, careening from coast to coast, and the spirit of movement imbued in the program appealed to me. So many weeks in Varanasi, off to New Delhi, up to Agra, down to Madras, it was exhilarating.

The spirit of service was appealing as well. Not only were we able to soak up the culture and history, we were able to give back to the disabled, the poor, the young.

My time in India was a profound experience. It developed in me a confidence I was able to take with me throughout the years. I have since spent considerable more time overseas, and have cultivated a career as an hotelier.

The story I tell most often about our trip to India happened on an impromptu trip up to Rishikesh, the mystic village of Beatles fame. We'd met a bit of resistance by the program director to spend our free weekend away from the class, but seven or eight of us decided to go anyhow. We left from New Delhi and arrived in the middle of the night, fortunately finding a guesthouse willing to take all of us into one room, four per bed. We only slept a couple of hours, because we woke to the distant outline of the Himalayas against the slowly lightening sky. We found our way to the Ghats, where ash stained sadhus was making morning ablutions. Up that high, the Ganges is a clean mountain stream, and we decided to brave the contaminants for the chance to wash away our sins and start anew. We met a rishi who told us of a temple complex high in the hills, so we hired a driver to brave the wending, pilgrim trodden roads. We made our offerings, and did some explorations, with one of the party noticing a small building high up on the hilltop. We climbed our way up past the ochre-robed monks, their ash-grey eyes and matted dreadlocks oblivious to us. As we came to the building I spied an ancient old man in white, his thin frail hand waving me over. I went to where he stood in front of a doorway to a small dark room beneath an altar. He motioned for me to enter, and bowing my head, I complied. He sat in front of me, and removed a spool of string, red and yellow, from somewhere within his robes. He took my wrist and tied the string around it, cutting it with a small blade that had been lying on the floor. He then asked me where I was from. "America," I replied. The smile that had been lingering softly in his eyes the whole time now burned fulgent. "America!" he cried. "Goooooood! We need more from America!" He looked on me with such warmth, such joy, such present awareness; I knew I had found a truly holy man. I used my rudimentary Hindi to get his name; Bhagawan Giri—The Singer of God. We spent the afternoon on the hill with the Baba, one by one receiving his benediction. He sent his boy for sweets and shared with us some of the most amazing hashish I've had the pleasure of smoking. When one of us commented on the beauty of the valley below, Bhagawan Giri smiled broadly and replied, "Tell it." The smile in his eyes was so knowing and playful, so wise and kind, that to this day, fifteen years later, I still try and cultivate it. I can spend a lifetime trying as I'm sure he did, and hopefully, one day, impart that same knowing smile, that same kind radiance, on another wayfaring child."

SUZANNE MILLER

The year was 1995. I was a professor in teacher education at the State University of New York, College at Oneonta, due for a sabbatical leave for one semester the following year. When Ashok Malhotra, a philosophy professor whose office was next to mine, asked if I would be interested in serving as his Assistant Director to SUNY Semester in India. He knew that I had served as a Peace Corps Volunteer in Micronesia and that I had involved my students in service learning in my teacher education courses. He wanted to build a service learning component into the India program he had been directing for many years. I was thrilled at this opportunity and scrapped all prior sabbatical plans to say,

"Yes, I would love to go!" Thus began a life journey unlike any other.

One of the first students I met who would be part of the program was Josie Basile, an older student at our college. I was impressed by her enthusiasm, her desire to learn, her intensity, and her compassion as she learned about the extreme poverty in India and how the children suffered. She decided to create the Children's India Fund and spent the summer prior to the trip raising money in a variety of ways. These included a spaghetti dinner, a booth at the local Firefighters' Carnival, and t-shirt sales. I admired her focus, her boundless energy and her commitment to this endeavor.

In September we left for India, which I found to be a fascinating country—a feast for the senses with its engaging and colorful sights, beautiful music, delicious food, diverse cultures and religions, and leaders such as Gandhi to be revered. But even my Peace Corps experience did not prepare me for the extreme poverty we witnessed in India. The initial weeks were especially difficult; I spent many hours in the early weeks talking with Josie who felt overwhelmed by what she saw. From the beginning she reached out to help, such as saving some of her food from meals to share with a homeless family who lived across the street from our hotel.

Our travels took us to the village of Dundlod in Rajasthan where we planned to spend our period of service and use some of the money that Josie had raised over the summer in a service project there. When village leaders, Ganga and Kunwar Raghuvendra Singh, said a school was needed for the poorest children who were unschooled because of the caste system, I was delighted at their choice. I had previously had a wonderful experience in starting the first Head Start preschool program in Chuuk, Micronesia, as a Peace Corps Volunteer, and was ready to apply my energy, knowledge and skills to help create this school for the underprivileged children in this village in India.

Josie Basile, Ashok Malhotra, the Singh's, and I worked to make the school become a reality. There was an empty building of one room which was donated as space. We hired two people from the village and I worked with them on some of the basics of good early childhood education. Learning materials such as slates and books were purchased and film canisters were gathered from the college students to use as manipulative materials to learn math. The word went out in the village and on the first day throngs of children turned up at the door of the school. We only had space for fifty and we decided to limit it to the primary grades. Sadly some had to be turned away. It was an emotional experience for me as I watched children who had never been in a classroom soak up all there was to learn and do. In all my previous decades of teaching, I have never seen children so eager and excited to learn.

We also involved the parents in the school and people from different castes sat together for the first time as parents met with village leaders. Toward the end of our stay in the village as I watched the children highly involved in learning tasks on the floor of their classroom, I looked at Josie across the room with tears in my eyes and I thought "Wow, we started a school!!" The seed had been planted. The dream had become a reality.

And now 15 years later, that school has grown from fifty children in one room with two teachers to 550 students and 18 staff members in a brand new building that includes a high school. Some of those first students have gone onto college. I had the privilege of returning to India for the 10th anniversary celebration of the school. It was a heart-warming event. Ashok Malhotra cut the ribbon for the new high school, speeches were given and the children performed songs and dances and dramatic skits. I was asked to address the audience of parents and village leaders about my reflections on the school's beginnings. What a joy it was to me to see how far we had come from our one room school 10 years ago.

Through her spiritual journey, so beautifully described in her book, Josie Basile planted the seed that helped to start a school in this desert village in northern India. Ashok Malhotra and his partner, Linda Drake, watered the "plant" and helped it grow through the Ninash Foundation that he established to help underprivileged children in India. Like a pebble dropped in a pond, the establishment of this school has had a rippling effect. Other individuals and nonprofit organizations from several countries have become involved in their support of our Indo-International School in Dundlod in various ways over the years. The Ninash Foundation has gone on to establish two more schools in India, one in Kuran, a village devastated by an earthquake, and an art restoration school in Mahapura.

I am now retired from teaching at SUNY Oneonta. As I look back on my various life experiences from serving as Peace Corps Volunteer on a small Pacific island where I have returned several times, to teaching Head Start in New York City, to developing and coordinating the early childhood teacher education program at SUNY Oneonta, my experience in India stands out as a life-changing one. People often think that they have no power to make a difference in the world. Josie's story demonstrates that we have the power to make a big difference and how we can inspire others to do the same.

Suzanne Miller, Ph.D., is Associate Professor Emerita at the State University of New York College at Oneonta where she developed the early childhood teacher education program and taught for 28 years. She has published several articles in teacher education journals related to service learning and was the 2007 Recipient of the Charles C Mackay, Jr. Excellence in Service Leadership Award.

The empty castle without my fellow travelers.

Children at the new Indo-International School, 2006.

DEDICATION

People often ask me why I dedicated my book to two people who have passed away and not to members of my family or close friends. My family and friends, of course, have been a constant presence and source of strength. They are honored by me every day of my life. There are people that come in and out of one's life that leave a strong residue of their presence. Joseph Fioravanti and Katherine Marshall are two of those people. My connection and significance with Katherine is stated at the beginning of this book. Joe's friendship is just as significant.

Joe had been my college professor at Delhi University when I was eighteen years old. There I sat front and center when this little man with a full beard, who looked more like Santa than an English Professor, walked in. He opened my world to the love of literature and foreign films, but our connection is far deeper.

Years later, I was married and living in Oneonta. I would run into Joe and his wife Shirley, they were also living there. We became friends.

I would tell Joe of my spiritual experiences and he would listen with interest. One day Joe said, "You should write your experiences down. You may want to share them with others someday." He was confirming what I already knew.

When I completed my first small version of this book, I called Joe and said, "I have written my experiences down. Can you take a look at them?"

A few weeks later Joe and I got together and he said, "There is a distinct voice in this book that wants to be heard."

His words echoed in my head for a year and I knew that I

would eventually have to release the voice. My friend passed away before he had a chance to see the completed book but I know that somehow, someway he has.

This book is dedicated to him for his friendship and encouragement over the years and his belief that I had something to say that wanted to be heard.

Joseph Fioravanti, my friend & mentor.

A GIFT FOR GIUSEPPA

Holly Martin read this book and was inspired to write this poem. Holly is a teaching instructor at Oneonta Job Corps.

A Gift for Giuseppa
In a time and place that exists by all,
Entered the world a little girl so small.
So many faces and experiences did she see,
She asked herself,
"God, do you have a gift for me?"

It wasn't until she was older,
That God spoke to her and told her.
She had a gift that was told by Him,
"To love them all as I would them."

Not knowing what her gift would mean,
She did the will of God unseen.
The gift embraced the future for all to see,
Be it All because of His Majesty.

It was by those who were not suppose to be touched,
That love was felt so much.
This was the Omega, especially from Him,
Others helped and did pitch in.
It was more than money that she gave,
It was a promise of a future, sure to change.

Her gift was given of her time and love,
Which embodied the light and maker above.

Later again she went back,
For a mission and plea to her pact.
Asking others to step up, feed the hungry and the poor,
Why me Lord? Please open some doors.

Doors were opened and His work was done,
And people around the world helped her fund.
The seed she planted by God's grace,
Has been watered by others as souls embraced.

Through humanity, oneness, giving and peace,
Giuseppa's passion did not cease.
Through grandeur ides and plans,
A molded piece of clay in His hands.

God's the master of it all,
The journey of souls together at last.
For these are the memories of Giuseppa's past,
It's amazing how life unfolds
from the help of someone big to the girl so small.

I hope that after reading this book it will give you thought to pause and reflect upon your own journey. I would like to hear from you concerning your own spiritual experiences to be included in future publications. I would be happy to be part of your book club by participating in Skype. You can reach me at the following e-mail for further information.

giuseppa333@gmail.com

Mama Giuseppa
4 South Liberty Avenue
Endicott, New York 13760

Josie Giuseppa Basile